Background and Purpose

The National Water Program Guidance for fiscal year (FY) 2012 describes how the U.S. Environmental Protection Agency (EPA), states, and tribal governments will work together to protect and improve the quality of the nation's water, including wetlands, and ensure safe drinking water (U.S. EPA, 2011). The Guidance describes the key actions needed to accomplish the public health and environmental goals proposed in the EPA 2011-2015 Strategic Plan (U.S. EPA, 2010). One goal is to protect public health by making finfish and shellfish safer to eat. Note that, unless otherwise specified, "fish" refers to both finfish and shellfish. One of the primary risks from eating fish is exposure to methylmercury (MeHg). In the U.S., exposure to MeHg in humans is largely through the consumption of fish (NRC, 2000). Mercury released into the environment is converted to MeHg in sediments and in the water column and bioaccumulates through aquatic food webs. This bioaccumulation leads to increased levels of MeHg in larger, older, predatory fish; concentrations in fish tissue may exceed a million fold the concentrations in water (NRC, 2000). MeHg exposure *in utero* is associated with adverse health effects, e.g., neurodevelopmental deficits such as IQ and motor function deficits in children (Mergler et al, 2007; NRC, 2000). In 2004 the FDA and EPA issued consumer advice. The advisory offers advice on amounts of commercial fish and fish from local water bodies that are safe to consume. This report investigates national trends over time in both blood mercury concentrations and fish consumption for women 16-49 years of age.

The EPA's approach to making fish safer to eat includes several key elements:

- Encourage development of statewide mercury reduction strategies.

- Reduce air deposition of mercury.

- Improve public information and notification of fish contamination risks.

One of the specific measures the Agency uses to estimate progress associated with this goal is blood mercury concentrations in women-of-childbearing age as reported by the Centers for Disease Control and Prevention's (CDC) National Center for Health Statistics (NCHS) in the National Health and Nutrition Examination Survey (NHANES). Blood total mercury (THg) concentrations reflect exposure to organic mercury, predominantly MeHg, from consumption of fish (Bjornberg et al. 2003; Sanzo et al. 2001; Svensson et al. 1992). NHANES is a continuing survey designed to collect data on the health and nutritional status of the U.S. population. The NHANES reports include information on chemicals or their metabolites as measured in blood samples collected from a statistically representative sample of the U.S. population. CDC releases the NHANES data every two years and reports environmental exposure results every two years in the National Report on Human Exposure to Environmental Chemicals (CDC, 2010a).

EPA developed a methodology to assess trends over time in the NHANES blood mercury data. This methodology was peer reviewed. Comments and concerns about the methodology received by the peer reviewers were addressed and the methodology was revised. The analyses discussed in this report use this revised methodology.

Previous work on blood mercury trends includes the publication by Mahaffey, Clickner, and Jeffries (2009), who analyzed NHANES 1999-2004 data for evidence of trends in blood mercury levels in women aged 16-49 years. The authors found no statistically significant difference among the three sets of study years (1999-2000, 2001-2002, and 2003-2004) for blood Hg, estimated 30-day Hg intake, or reported frequency of fish consumption. However, in multiple regression modeling, adjusting for covariates including coastal/non-coastal residence, women aged 16-49 who participated in the years 1999-2000 had significantly higher blood Hg levels compared with those who participated in 2003-2004. Women who participated in 2001-2002 had significantly lower blood Hg levels than those who participated in 2003-2004. Although the analyses did not support the conclusion that there was a general downward trend in blood Hg concentrations over the 6-year study period, there was a decline in the upper percentiles reflecting the most highly exposed women with blood Hg concentrations greater than established levels of concern. They observed a decrease in the 90th percentile of 30-day estimated intake of Hg through fish consumption across the six study years even though there was no similar decrease in the 90th percentile of 30-day estimated consumption of grams of fish. This suggested a shift in consumption to fish containing less Hg. They did not observe a similar pattern at the mean, suggesting that this shift in fish consumption occurred mainly with the highest fish consumers.

Caldwell, et al., 2009, reported finding no differences across NHANES study years in blood total mercury concentrations for the subpopulation of women 16-49 years in NHANES 1999-2006, after adjusting for age and race/ethnicity (p=0.11).

The goals of this report are to investigate differences over time in blood mercury concentrations in women of child-bearing age using NHANES 1999-2010 data and to investigate changes in fish consumption and mercury intake over time. This report documents an analysis of the 1999-2010

NHANES data on the distribution of blood mercury concentrations and the association of these with time, age, sex, race/ethnicity, income, and fish consumption. Regression analysis was used to assess whether or not there are significant differences in blood mercury concentrations across the six study segments (1999-2000, 2001-2002, 2003-2004, 2005-2006, 2007-2008, 2009-2010) based on national estimates, after adjustment for fish consumption and demographic covariates known to be associated with blood mercury concentrations (Schober et al., 2003; Mahaffey et al., 2004; Mahaffey et al., 2009; Caldwell et al., 2009). Additional analysis was done to assess whether or not there are significant differences in fish consumption and mercury intake across the study period.

Methods 2

2.1 Methods Overview

Previous research on blood mercury indicates that the predictors of blood mercury concentrations include fish consumption, age, race/ethnicity, income, and other variables. There are two sources of information on dietary fish intake in the NHANES data. One source is the 24-hour recall data with information on the quantity of food consumed and the second source is the report of 30-day frequency of consumption of selected fish species. These were combined to produce useful estimates of the amounts of fish consumed by a participant. These estimates were used to develop population-based statistics on fish consumption

The analysis also combined NHANES measurements of blood mercury with NHANES measurements of fish consumption and measurements of mercury concentrations in fish to investigate the relationship between mercury intake from fish and blood MeHg concentrations across six NHANES survey releases covering 12 years. The following sections describe the data and the analysis procedures. All data processing and analyses were performed using the Statistical Analysis System (SAS) version 9.2 (SAS Institute, 2010).

2.2 NHANES Data Overview

The required NHANES data files and variables were identified and downloaded from the NHANES website (CDC 2010a). These files were then merged to create a dataset customized to the needs of this project. For each NHANES survey release, the required data are in the following files:

- Demographics - gender, age, race/ethnicity, education, income, sampling weights, pseudo-stratum, and pseudo-primary sampling unit (PSU). The pseudo-stratum and pseudo-PSU variables provide information on how participants were selected and are needed to calculate standard errors and p-values. They are modified from the actual NHANES strata and PSUs for disclosure control, and are thus prefixed "pseudo."

- Laboratory results - blood total mercury concentration and blood inorganic mercury concentration.

4

- Body measures - body weight.

- Dietary intake, 24 hour recall - food codes, meal name, amount eaten; one record per food item eaten.

- Dietary intake, 30 day frequency of consumption - number of times each of the following species was reported consumed in the previous 30 days: clams, crabs, crayfish, lobster, mussels, oysters, scallops, shrimp, other shellfish, other unknown shellfish, breaded fish products, tuna (not differentiated by canned light, canned white or steaks), bass, catfish, cod, flatfish, haddock, mackerel, perch, pike, pollock, porgy, salmon, sardines, sea bass, shark, swordfish, trout, walleye, other fish, and other unknown fish.

Over the six two-year periods from 1999 to 2010, NHANES has changed the scope of participants for some types of data collected. Table 2 summarizes these changes. Across survey releases, consistent data are available for children aged 1 to 5 and women aged 16 to 49. This analysis uses the data for women ages 16 to 49. Note there were no differences pertinent to this analysis between 2005 and 2010.

Table 2.   Scope of data collection by data type and survey release

Data Type	NHANES Survey Release			
	1999-2000	2001-2002	2003-2004	2005-2010
Blood mercury	Both sexes aged 1-5 years, women aged 16-49 years	Both sexes aged 1-5 years, women aged 16-49 years	Both sexes aged 1 year and older	Both sexes aged 1 year and older
Demographics	All participants	All participants	All participants	All participants
Body weight	All participants	All participants	All participants	All participants
Fish consumed, 30-day frequency	Both sexes aged 1 year and older	Both sexes aged 1-5 years, women aged 16-49 years	Both sexes aged 1-5 years, women aged 16-49 years	Both sexes aged 1 year and older
Diet, 24-hr intake	All participants, one day's intake	All participants, one day's intake	All participants, two days' intake (second day by phone)	All participants, two days' intake (second day by phone)

The relevant files were downloaded from the NHANES website. The unique identifier variable "SEQN" was used to link the data on each participant from different data sets. The analysis was performed following the NHANES Analytical Guidelines posted on the NHANES website (CDC 2010b). The sample sizes – number of unique SEQN's for women aged 16-49 with data for this study-- for each of these files are in Table 3. The sample sizes vary by NHANES survey release due to sample design changes over time and because some participants failed to provide all of the requested information. The final row of the table indicates the sample size used in the analyses contained in this report.

Table 3.   Number of participating women aged 16-49 by data file and survey release

Number of participants (unique SEQN)	1999-00	2001-02	2003-04	2005-06	2007-08	2009-10	Total, 1999-2010
Demographic file	1,944	2,140	1,900	2,085	1,749	1,996	11,814
Blood Hg[1]	1,707	1,906	1,704	1,873	1,583	1,868	10,641
Body weight	1,809	1,966	1,802	1,992	1,681	1,939	11,189
Diet (24-h)[2]	1,732	1,933	1,722	1,920	1,625	1,865	10,797
Diet(30-d)[2]	1,731	1,931	1,721	1,918	1,625	1,864	10,790
All Data Elements of Interest	1,637	1,780	1,599	1,792	1,493	1,786	10,087

[1]One outlier was removed from the analysis dataset
[2]Counts of participants whose dietary recall status was reliable and met minimum criteria by NHANES

2.3   Blood Total and Inorganic Mercury Concentration Data

The laboratory data files contain total mercury and inorganic mercury. Table 4 summarizes the laboratory methods used to analyze the blood samples for mercury.

In blood samples with low levels of mercury, total and/or inorganic mercury concentration measurements below the laboratory lower detection limit (LDL) are reported as less than the detection limit without providing a measured concentration. In the data files, the unspecified concentrations for these samples are replaced by a substitute value. For the analysis, the LDL was assumed to equal the substitute value in the data file times the square root of 2. This approach appears consistent with the stated procedure for 1999-2000 and with the distribution of the detected values. However, for total mercury in the 2007-2008 file, the substitute value times the square root of 2 is 0.28 and the smallest reported detected value is 0.33. To be consistent with the distribution of the reported values and because there are detected values of 0.33, the LDL was set to 0.325. Also, for the 1999-2000 data, the substitute value in the file is rounded to one digit after the decimal place; the calculations used the reported substitute value of 0.097 for total and 0.032 for inorganic mercury. The different and sometimes multiple substitute values suggest that different detection limits were applicable for different years or samples, contrary to what is implied by the reported LDL in Table 4.

Table 4.   Laboratory analysis methodology for blood total mercury and inorganic mercury

Parameter	Survey Release					
	1999-2000	2001-2002	2003-2004	2005-2006	2007-2008	2009-2010
Laboratory method[a]	Flow Injection Cold Vapor Atomic Absorption (CVAA) Method No.: 1190B/06-OD		Blood total mercury: ICPDRCMS Method No: ITB001A Blood inorganic mercury[e]: FIMS CVAA (formerly Flow Injection Cold Vapor Atomic Absorption (CVAA)). Method No: ITB003A (formerly:1190B/06-OD)	Blood total mercury: ICPDRCMS Method No: ITB001A Blood inorganic mercury: FIMS CVAA (formerly Flow Injection Cold Vapor Atomic Absorption (CVAA)). Method No: ITB003A (formerly:1190B/06-OD)	Blood total mercury: ICPDRCMS Method No: ITB001A Blood inorganic mercury: FIMS CVAA (formerly Flow Injection Cold Vapor Atomic Absorption (CVAA)). Method No: ITB003A (formerly:1190B/06-OD)	Blood total mercury: ICPDRCMS Method No: ITB001A Blood inorganic mercury: FIMS CVAA (formerly Flow Injection Cold Vapor Atomic Absorption (CVAA)). Method No: ITB003A (formerly:1190B/06-OD)
Data file	Lab06, l06_b		L06bmt_c	Thgigh_d	Thgihg_e	Thgigh_f
Reportable range[a]	LDL to 50 µg/L		Above LDL	LDL to 50 µg/L	LDL to 50 µg/L	LDL to 50 µg/L
Lower Detection Limits (LDL)[a]:						
Total Hg[aa]	0.137 µg/L (3*std of 10 runs of a low Hg level sample)		0.2[b] µg/L (3*std of >20 run of blood blank)	0.33[b] (3*std of >20 runs of blood blank)	Not specified (3*std of >20 runs of blood blank)	0.33 (3*std of >20 runs of blood blank)
Inorganic Hg[aa]	0.446 µg/L (3*std of 10 runs of a low Hg level sample)		0.446[c] µg/L(3*std of 10 runs of a low Hg level sample)	0.446 (3*std of 10 runs of a low Hg level sample)	0.446 µg/L(3*std of 10 runs of a low Hg level sample)	0.35 µg/L (3*std of 10 runs of a low Hg level sample)
Substitute value for results below the LDL[a]:	DL over square root of 2 Total Hg: 0.097 µg/L, Inorganic Hg: 0.32 µg/L	DL over square root of 2[b] Total Hg: 0.07 µg/L, Inorganic Hg: 0.28 µg/L	Total Hg: .1, .14 µg/L Inorganic Hg: .3 µg/L	Total Hg: .14, .23 µg/L Inorganic Hg: .25, .28 µg/L	Total Hg: 0.20 µg/L Inorganic: 0.25 µg/L	Total Hg: 0.23 µg/L Inorganic: 0.25 µg/L
BDL indicator[d]	NA		NA	LBDTHGLC, LBDIHGLC	LBDTHGLC, LBDIHGLC	LBDTHGLC, LBDIHGLC
No. of digits after the decimal	1		1	2	2	2
Eligible Participants	Both sexes ages 1-5, Females 16-49		Both sexes ages 1 - 150			

[a]Laboratory Method procedure documents are available on the NHANES website (http://www.cdc.gov/nchs/nhanes.htm).

[b]From Caldwell, K.L., et al., 2009

[c]Analytical method together with DL for inorganic Hg was not mentioned clearly in the method file. Based on the description in NHANES documentation, it uses the method with the DL cited.

[d]A variable that indicates if a measurement was below the limit of detection.

2.3.1 Adjustments for Non-Detects in Total and Inorganic Mercury

The analysis variable, blood MeHg concentration, is calculated by subtracting the inorganic mercury concentration from the total mercury concentration. However, 81 percent of the inorganic and 12 percent of the total mercury measurements are below the detection limit. Thus, for most participants the calculation of MeHg depends on how the non-detects are handled. Some methods for handling these values below the detection limit include substituting values equal to the detection limit over the square-root of 2, adapting survival analysis, and multiple imputation of the non-detects. Based on analysis of simulated data with characteristics similar to the NHANES data, multiple imputation was selected for analysis. Although more complicated than other alternatives, multiple imputation is the most flexible and yields significant improvement in the estimates of standard errors and p-values over other methods.

Multiple imputation involves imputing concentrations for the non-detect total and inorganic mercury measurements. Assuming the total and inorganic mercury concentrations have a lognormal distribution, the imputed concentrations are simulated values that 1) are less than the detection limit, 2) have the same correlation with other variables as do the non-censored values, and 3) have a lognormal distribution. The imputed MeHg was calculated from the imputed total and inorganic mercury concentrations. The imputation process involved the following steps: 1) use survival analysis (SAS LIFEREG procedure) to model the inorganic mercury concentrations as a function of total mercury concentration and other predictors; 2) simulate the inorganic mercury concentrations for non-detects based on the model results; 3) use survival analysis to model the total mercury concentrations as a function of inorganic mercury concentration and other predictors; 4) simulate the total mercury concentrations for non-detects, and 5) repeat the previous steps to create ten versions of the data, each with a different set of imputed values for the non-detects. Each version of the data was analyzed and the ten results were combined (using the SAS MIANALYZE procedure) to obtain the final estimates and standard errors, adjusted for the uncertainty associated with the imputation process.

2.3.2 Calculation of MeHg Concentration

Preliminary MeHg concentrations (M) are obtained by subtracting inorganic mercury concentrations from total mercury concentrations. Whether based on imputed or observed values, the calculated organic mercury concentration can be negative due to imprecision in the total and organic mercury measurements. As it is biologically impossible to have negative blood MeHg concentrations, and because biological measurements can often be described by a lognormal distribution, the calculated values were transformed to be positive, with an approximate lognormal distribution. The transformation that was used makes the negative measurements positive by adjusting up the negative concentrations the most, adjusting values near zero up somewhat, and leaving values much greater than zero relatively unchanged. This transformation has the advantage that values much above zero can be interpreted as MeHg concentrations and values closer to zero provide a plausible approximation to the MeHg concentration. The transformed values can be analyzed to identify predictors of MeHg levels even though the lower values provide only an approximation to the true concentration. However, estimates of lower percentiles of the distribution of MeHg concentrations are, at best, approximate.

In the following transformation, MeHg is the MeHg concentration used in the analysis and C is set to achieve a desired distribution for the log of the transformed data (approximately symmetric with skewness close to zero and roughly normally distributed).

$$MeHg = \left(\frac{M + \sqrt{M^2 + C}}{2} \right)$$

To incorporate the uncertainty in the selection of C into the analysis, a slightly different value of C was used for each imputed dataset. The skewness of the log-transformed MeHg values varied from -0.37 to 0.66 across the ten imputed data sets.

2.4   30-Day Consumption Frequency Data

The 30-day consumption frequency data include reports by participants concerning the number of times she consumed each of 31 types of fish, as listed in Section 2.1 of this report, in the previous 30 days. There are no data on the amounts eaten. About three-quarters of participants report eating some fish over the 30 days prior to the interview. These data, together with the 24-hour recall data, are used to develop estimates of 30-day fish consumption amounts. In later formulas, the consumption frequency data are designated as $EatFreq_{Person,Species}$.

2.5   24-Hour Dietary Recall Data

The 24-hour recall data include the U.S. Department of Agriculture (USDA) food codes from the Food and Nutrient Database for Dietary Studies (FNNDS) and amount consumed in grams for every item of food eaten by the participant in the 24 hours immediately preceding the interview. These FNDDS files are available from the Agriculture Research Service of the USDA (USDA, 2004; USDA, 2006; USDA, 2008; USDA 2010; Ahuja, et al., 2012). The recipes for the food codes were searched to find all food codes that contain finfish or shellfish. All records in the 24-hour data file for women aged 16-49 years that were for fish-containing food codes were extracted. Only about 15 percent of participants reported consuming fish on any one day. The recipe file and 24-hour recall data were merged to calculate quantity of raw fish consumed per recipe.

We fit a regression model using the SAS GLM procedure predicting the log-transformed quantity of raw fish consumed (grams, adjusted for cooking method and percentage of fish in the recipe) from the 24-hour file, as a function of number of times each species was consumed in the last 30 days, race/ethnicity, age, income, and NHANES survey release, keeping only significant predictors. The significant predictors were species, race/ethnicity, and log-transformed 30-day frequency of consumption as both a linear and squared term. The prediction equation from the fit was applied to the 30-day recall data to predict the geometric mean quantity of fish in a meal for each subject and species consumed in the last 30 days. This is designated as $\overline{MealSize}_{Person,species}$. The predicted value was used, even if a woman had reported grams from the 24-hour recall data for a species also reported consumed in the last 30 days. The details concerning adjustments due to cooking and preparation have been published in previous reports (U.S. EPA, 1997; Mahaffey et al., 2004).

For species with little or no data, the models combined data across species to predict the amount of fish consumed in a meal. The meal size for "Other fish" and "Other shellfish" was calculated from finfish or shellfish species that are present in the 24-hour file but not specifically reported on in the 30-day frequency of consumption file; these include species such as tilapia and eel for finfish, squid for shellfish, and other finfish and shellfish infrequently reported. For some species in the 30 day file there were no corresponding data in the 24-hour recall file. For those species a value from another species was used. Specifically, bass, porgy, and walleye used the quantities for salmon, "Breaded fish" used the quantities for pollock, shark used the quantities for swordfish, and "Shellfish not specified" used the quantities for scallop.

2.6 Fish Tissue Mercury Data

In order to estimate mercury intake, data on mercury concentrations in fish tissue are needed. Mercury concentration in fish varies greatly among species and within species, with older and larger fish having higher concentrations (U.S. EPA, 1997). Previous analyses (Mahaffey et al., 2004 and

Mahaffey et al., 2009) used the fish tissue concentration data reported in the 1997 Mercury Study Report to Congress (U.S. EPA, 1997). Much of the data in that report are from the National Marine Fisheries Service 1978 database. As it is possible that mercury concentrations in fish tissue have changed over the past few decades, we updated these values. For most species consumed by women aged 16-49 years in the NHANES data 1999-2010, we were able to find data that corresponds to this time period. However, for two species we were not able to locate more recent data and used data from before 1998. These species are abalone and crayfish. The data we obtained represented sampling of over 26,000 fish.

We obtained data on mercury concentration in fish tissue from the following sources:

- Alaska Department of Environmental Conservation, Fish Tissue Testing Program;

- Surface Water Ambient Monitoring Program, State of California;

- Florida Marine Research Institute, Florida Fish and Wildlife Conservation Commission;

- Department of Environmental Conservation, New York State;

- State of Tennessee;

- State of Virginia;

- State of Massachusetts;

- Micro Analytical Systems, Inc.;

- Burger and Gochfeld, 2006 (data from fish in Chicago, Illinois supermarkets);

- U.S. FDA;

- State of Arkansas, Department of Environmental Quality;

- Lake Michigan Mass Balance Study;

- Contaminants in Fish from California Lakes and Reservoirs, State of California Water Resources Control Board;

- McKelvey et al., 2010 (data from New York City Asian fish markets);

- Tsuchiya et al., 2008 (data from Asian grocery stores in the Puget Sound area);

- McBride, 2005 (data from store-bought fish in Washington State);

- Report to Congress (U.S. EPA, 1997);

- Health Canada (Health Canada, 2008);

- National Rivers and Streams Assessment (data from U.S. EPA); and

- State of Louisiana Department of Environmental Quality.

To estimate the geometric mean mercury concentration for each fish species, we used the SAS MIXED procedure and modeled the log-transformed fish tissue mercury concentration by fish species, treating the data source as a random effect. Some of the data sources reported average concentrations for multiple fish samples and some sources reported mercury concentrations for each individual fish sampled. In order to account for this in the modeling, we included a weighting factor. The weighting factor allowed the modeling to take into account differing variances due to both data source and number of individual fish samples contributing to each reported value, modeling the error variance as a power function of the number of samples averaged to obtain the reported value. The predicted values were converted to geometric mean fish mercury concentrations, designated as $\overline{FishHg}_{Species}$. The average mercury concentration weighted by 30-day consumption frequency was used for "Fish not specified" and "Shellfish not specified" species. To the extent it could be tested, there were no consistent time trends in the fish mercury concentration data in the sources that we used. The mercury concentrations used in the analyses by species are in Table A-1.

2.7   Estimation of 30-Day Fish Consumption and Mercury Intake

Estimates of the amounts of fish consumed over 30 days were calculated by combining the two NHANES consumption data sets – the 24-hour recall data and the 30-day frequency of consumption data. Basically, the 24-hour data provide the amount consumed at one time. The 30-day frequency data provide the number of times fish was consumed in past 30-days. Because many women who reported consuming fish in the previous 30 days did not have data for fish consumption in the 24-hour data (they did not consume fish in the past 24 hours), we needed to estimate the amount they consume during a meal in order to calculate their estimated 30 day consumption.

The predicted values of the amount of fish consumed at one time for each species from the modeling were multiplied by the number of times the participant reported consuming that species in the previous 30 days. The resulting values for each of the 31 species were then summed for each participant to yield the estimated 30-day consumption of fish for each woman aged 16-49 years that completed the NHANES dietary data collection. In the formula below, FSSpecies corresponds to the 31 fish species in the 30-day recall data. Similar calculations were made to obtain the grams of finfish and grams of shellfish consumed.

$$GramsFS_{Person} = \sum_{FSSpecies} EatFreq_{Person,Species} \times \overline{MealSize}_{Person,species}$$

To calculate the estimated 30-day mercury intake from fish, the predicted amount of fish consumed at one time for each species from the modeling was also multiplied by the predicted mercury concentration for the species and the number of times the participant reported consuming that species in the previous 30 days.

$$HgIntakeFS_{Person} = \sum_{FSSpecies} EatFreq_{Person,Species} \times \overline{MealSize}_{Person,species} \times \overline{FishHg}_{Species}$$

The reference dose (RfD) of MeHg of 0.1 ug/kg per day, is adjusted for body weight. Thus, in order to present data that can be easily compared to the RfD, we adjusted the estimates of mercury intake by body weight. We divided the 30-day estimate of mercury intake by body weight to get the body weight adjusted estimates.

As demonstrated by the following equations, the mercury intake per body weight can be expressed as the product of four components corresponding to: 1) frequency of fish consumption; 2) weighted average meal size, weighted by frequency of consumption; 3) weighted average fish tissue mercury concentration, weighted by the quantity of fish consumed; and 4) inverse body weight.

$$HgIntakeFSPerKg_{Person} =$$

$$\frac{\sum_{FSSpecies} EatFreq_{Person,Species} \times \overline{MealSize}_{Person,species} \times \overline{FishHg}_{Species}}{BodyKG_{Person}}$$

$$= \sum_{FSSpecies} EatFreq_{Person,Species}$$

$$\times \frac{\sum_{FSSpecies} EatFreq_{Person,Species} \times \overline{MealSize}_{Person,species}}{\sum_{FSSpecies} EatFreq_{Person,Species}}$$

$$\times \frac{\sum_{FSSpecies} EatFreq_{Person,Species} \times \overline{MealSize}_{Person,species} \times \overline{FishHg}_{Species}}{\sum_{FSSpecies} EatFreq_{Person,Species} \times \overline{MealSize}_{Person,species}}$$

$$\times \frac{1}{BodyKg_{Person}}$$

Logistic regression was used to model the probability of consuming fish in a 30-day period, and for those that consumed fish (consumers), regression analysis was used to model these four components, predicting the log-transformed values.

2.8   Statistical Analysis Methods

The distributions of blood mercury, frequency of fish consumption, 30-day estimates of fish consumption, and 30-day estimates of mercury intake for the female NHANES participants aged 16-49 years were calculated. Analyses were carried out for both blood THg and blood MeHg because while MeHg is the preferred analysis variable, due to the high percentage of samples with inorganic mercury concentrations below the LDL, analysis of THg may provide more robust results. Box plots were created to display the distributions of blood THg and blood MeHg. In these plots the bottom and top edges of the box correspond to the 25th and 75th percentiles. The difference between these is the intra-quartile range (IQR). The diamond inside the box indicates the geometric mean value and the line inside the box indicates the median value. The whiskers that extend from each box indicate the range of values that are within 1.5*IQR of the end of the box. Any points that are a distance of more than 1.5*IQR from the box are indicated on the box plots as circles. The width of the box is proportional to the number of participants in each category.

Blood THg and blood MeHg were both analyzed for evidence of trends over the period from 1999 to 2010. Detailed tables of blood THg and blood MeHg concentrations were generated, giving sample sizes, arithmetic means, and percentiles (25th, 50th, 75th, 90th, and 95th), and their 95% confidence intervals, by survey release, age, income, and race/ethnicity. These tables are in the Appendix. Analytical extracts of these tabulations, generally graphic, are presented in the body of the report. For presentation purposes, age was categorized into four groups, 16-19, 20-29, 30-39, and 40-49 years old. Race/ethnicity groups recorded in NHANES include Mexican American, Other Hispanic, Non-Hispanic White, Non-Hispanic Black, and Other Race. Other Race consists of Asian, Native American, Pacific and Caribbean Islander, Alaska Native, multiracial, and unknown race. Household income categories are reported somewhat differently across the six NHANES survey releases. In addition, income is elicited using two sets of questions, the first for less than or greater than $20K and the second with a more detailed breakdown. For the analysis, the income categories reflect the available data rather than a set of ordered categories. The income categories used for the analysis are: less than $20K, $20-45K, $45-75K, greater than $75K, greater than $20K but not otherwise specified, Refused or Don't Know combined into one category due to small sample size, and a category for multiple family household for which the household income was not calculated.

Similar analyses were performed for per capita frequency of fish consumption, estimated amounts of fish consumed, and estimated mercury intake, to look for possible trends in fish consumption. Then, blood MeHg levels were analyzed with respect to the 30-day frequencies of consumption, with detailed tables in the Appendix and extracts in the body of the report.

All analyses were performed following the NHANES Analytical Guidelines posted on the NHANES website (CDC 2010b). In particular, this means that all analyses were weighted using the statistical weights recommended in the Analytical Guidelines, that is, the MEC weights. The sampling design variables were used in calculating the variance of the estimates by 1) creating a set of Balanced Repeated Replication (BRR) replicate weights with a Fay factor of 0.3; and 2) using the SAS survey procedures (SURVEYMEANS, SURVEYREG, SURVEYFREQ) or equivalent procedures with the replicate weights. The BRR weights were created to facilitate fitting the non-linear model described below and, for consistency, used for all the estimates. For the analysis of imputed concentrations (blood THg or blood MeHg), the estimates were calculated using each imputed dataset and combined using the SAS MIANALYZE procedure to obtain standard errors and p-values that account for the uncertainty associated with the imputation process.

2.8.1   Calculation of Percentiles

Percentiles were estimated using linear interpolation in the inverted sample cumulative probability distribution such that bias was minimized (Hyndman and Fan, 1996; Rogers, 2003). The confidence intervals around the percentile estimates were estimated using the Woodruff method (Sarndal, Swenson, and Wretman, 1992).

2.8.2   Regression Analysis Predicting Blood Mercury Concentrations

Using the SAS NLIN procedure, non-linear regression analysis was used to model the relationship between blood MeHg and mercury intake from fish, adjusting for differences by participant age, race, income, and time across NHANES survey release. The analysis used the BRR replicate weights and the imputed MeHg values. The resulting standard errors reflect the uncertainty due to imputation.

15

The model assumes a linear relationship between 30-day mercury intake from fish and the blood MeHg concentration. Linear regression assumes the prediction errors have constant variance. However, the variance of the MeHg concentrations increases as the mercury intake increases and the variance is fairly constant for the log-transformed MeHg concentration. This suggests using the following non-linear model where the error (n) is assumed to be normally distributed with constant variance:

$$ln(MeHg) = ln(Intercept + Slope \times HgIntake) +$$

Since the MeHg concentration may vary by other factors, such as income, race, age, body weight, and year of the NHANES survey release, the following model was fit:

$$ln(MeHg) = ln(Intercept + Slope \times HgIntake) + Income_i + Race_r + ln\left(\frac{Age}{29}\right)$$
$$+ \left(ln\left(\frac{Age}{29}\right)\right)^2 + ln\left(\frac{Bodyweight}{76}\right) + Diff1999 + YrTrend + YrQuadratic$$
$$+ n$$

Income and race are represented by dummy variables, where the subscript indexes the income or race category. Dummy variables can be formulated in different ways. The dummy variables for income and race were created using deviations-from-the-mean coding (also referred to as effect level coding). Using race with five categories as an example, assume the mean MeHg for the five categories, after adjusting for other effects, is Mean1, Mean2, Mean3, Mean4, and Mean5. The parameter for category 1(for example) is the difference between Mean1 and the mean of Mean1, Mean2, Mean3, Mean4, and Mean5. As a result, the parameters sum to zero. The model is fit using only four dummy variables and the parameter for the fifth category (the reference category) is equal to the negative of the sum of the parameters for the other categories. The mean of the five parameters (Mean1 through Mean5) represents the mean for a population which is evenly distributed across the five race categories. In the discussion of results, this will be referred to as the response for a typical participant. The parameter estimates and standard errors can be used to assess whether the mean or geometric mean for a selected race category and the mean or geometric mean for a typical participant are significantly different. In the non-log measurement units, the income and race parameters correspond to multiplicative differences in the MeHg concentration between categories. The analysis tables show the estimate for the reference category and an overall F-test across all levels of the categorical variables.

The effect of age on ln(MeHg) was modeled using two variables representing a quadratic relationship in ln(age). In order to be able to interpret the parameter estimates and p-values for the two age terms independently, age was scaled by dividing by 29 before taking the log. This makes the linear and quadratic terms essentially uncorrelated. An overall F-test across the two age variables is also calculated.

Although body weight is a component of mercury intake per body weight, there may be addition differences associated with body weight. In the model, body weight is scaled by dividing by 76 before taking the log; 76 kilograms equals 168 pounds. Although not used in the model, scaling by 76 would make the correlation between log-transformed body weight and its square roughly zero.

In preliminary analyses, the blood THg and MeHg levels appear to decrease between the 1999-2000 NHANES release and subsequent releases. However, there is not a corresponding change in the mercury intake or fish consumption estimates. As a result, the statistical modeling in this report focuses on trends in blood mercury concentrations since the 1999-2000 release while including the 1999-2000 data in the analysis. The effect of time (Year of NHANES data release) on ln(MeHg) is represented by three terms for: a) a linear trend after 2000; b) a quadratic trend after 2000; and c) the difference between the mean for the 1999-2000 NHANES release and the mean for releases after 2000. These three variables for assessing time differences were constructed to be essentially uncorrelated so that the parameters and p-values could be interpreted independently. These variables are centered to have a mean close to zero. An overall F-test across all three time variables is also calculated. Also, the quadratic relationship from data after 2000 was extrapolated backwards to assess if the average from the 1999-2000 release is different from what would be expected based on the trend across later years.

The interpretation of the model parameters is complicated due to the complexity of the model, how the dummy variables were created, and measurement error. With the provision that MeHg levels vary by race and income, the intercept and slope can be interpreted as an approximate estimate of geometric mean MeHg concentration and the increase in MeHg per unit increase in mercury intake per body weight for a typical women 29 years old weighing 76 kilograms. Note however, that the parameters are affected by the selected imputation procedures. Also, if essentially all MeHg comes from fish consumption, then we would expect the terms for differences by income, race, and age to be insignificant. However, the available measures of meal size, fish mercury concentration, and frequency of fish consumption are imprecise. These quantities are related to income, race, and age. As a result, it is likely that the income, race, and age differences found in the model are, at least in part, explaining differences in blood MeHg and THg that are not adequately explained by the imprecise estimate of mercury intake.

2.8.3   Logistic Regression Predicting MeHg > 5.8 µg/L

Logistic regression was used to predict the probability that the blood MeHg concentration is greater than 5.8 µg/L and evaluate whether the probability of high MeHg values has decreased over the 12 years covered by the data. Using a safety factor of 10, the blood MeHg value of 5.8 µg/L is one tenth of the lower 95 percent confidence limit of the cord blood mercury concentration associated with neurologic effects on the fetus (NRC, 2000). Additionally, a blood MeHg value of 5.8 µg/L is the concentration that forms the basis for the EPA RfD for MeHg (Rice et al., 2000). The model used the same predictors as the nonlinear model described above except that the non-linear term involving two parameters $(ln(Intercept + Slope \times HgIntake))$ was replaced by an intercept and the transformed fish mercury intake per body weight derived from the nonlinear model described in Section 2.8.2 above. The transformation used is the corresponding term from the non-linear fit resulting in the following logistic model where b is a binomial error:

$$logit(MeHg) = Intercept + Slope1 \times ln(0.4388 + 1.0492 HgIntake) + Income_i + Race_r$$
$$+ ln\left(\frac{Age}{29}\right) + \left(ln\left(\frac{Age}{29}\right)\right)^2 + ln\left(\frac{Bodyweight}{76}\right) + Diff1999 + YrTrend$$
$$+ YrQuadratic + b$$

2.8.4   Modeling Factors Contributing to Mercury Intake

As noted in Section 2.7, the mercury intake per body weight from fish can be expressed as the product of four components described briefly as: frequency of consumption, meal size, fish mercury concentration, and inverse body weight. For those that consumed fish, the log-transformed mercury intake per body weight is the sum of the log-transformed components. In order to assess a linear time trend in each of these components (represented by Y) the following model was used:

$$ln(Y) = Intercept + Income_i + Race_r + Age_a + YrTrend +$$

These results are presented in the appendix. However, to facilitate presentation of the results, the parameters from the following model (treating all predictors as categorical) are shown in the plots:

$$ln(Y) = Intercept + Income_i + Race_r + Age_a + Year_y +$$

As described above, dummy variables for the categorical levels were created using deviations-from-the-mean coding. In addition, logistic regression was used to predict the probability of reporting any fish consumption in the previous 30 days (using the variable AteFish30). These models used the same predictors as above for predicting Logit(AteFish30).

2.8.5   Trends

When not otherwise specified, trends in continuous variables were assessed using regression with only one predictor, year of NHANES survey release. Trends in percentiles were assessed using logistic regression to test if the proportion above or below the overall percentile varies linearly by year. This approach provides a general assessment of trends. However, regression adjustments for other possible differences over time, as when using the non-linear model, can provide a more precise assessment of trends.

3.1 Trends in Blood Mercury Concentrations

The distribution of blood THg and blood MeHg, both measured as µg Hg/L blood (µg/L) was first examined for evidence of temporal trends. Figures 1 and 2 display the distributions for blood THg and blood MeHg, respectively, using boxplots.

Figure 1.   **Distribution of blood THg (µg/L), by NHANES survey release, women aged 16-49 years**

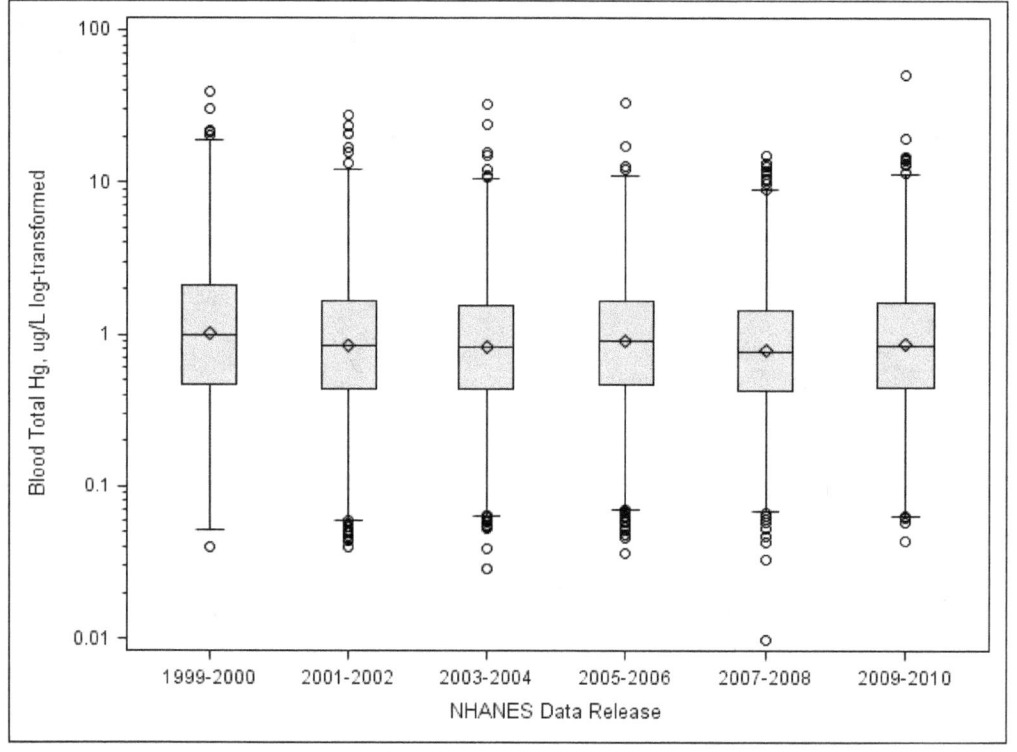

Figure 2. Distribution of blood MeHg (µg/L), by NHANES survey release, women aged 16-49 years

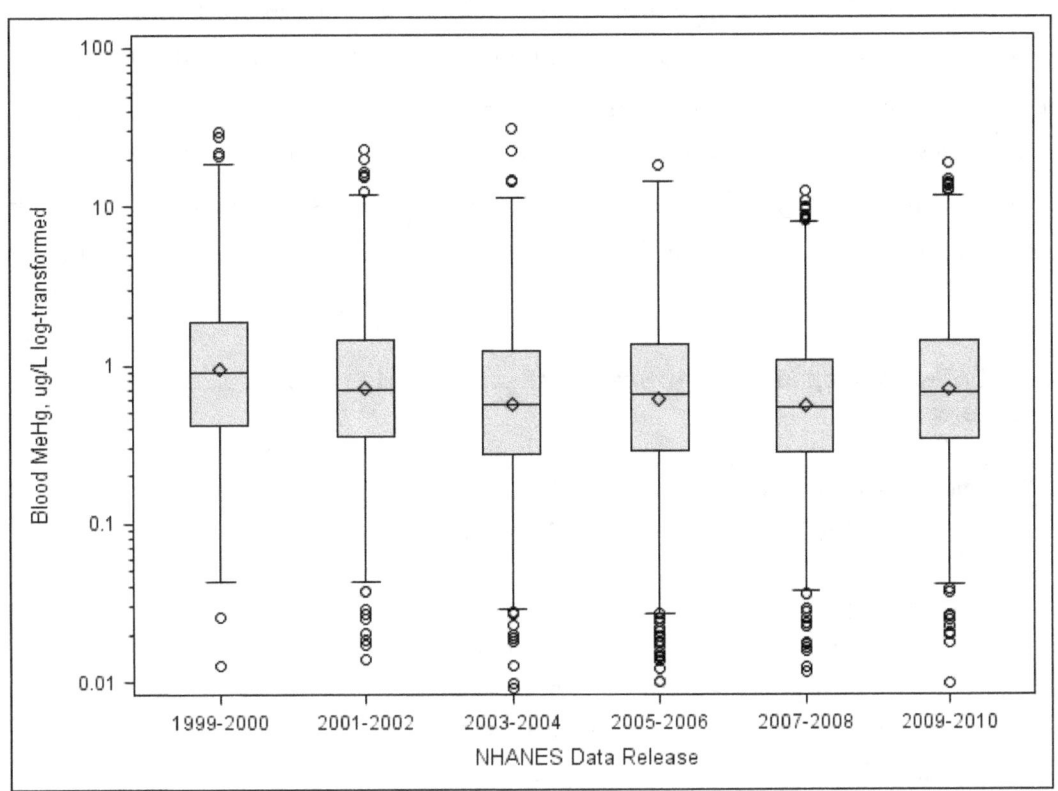

The figures show similar patterns across time; however the MeHg plot shows larger differences in the means between years. The geometric mean blood THg in 1999-2000 was 1.21 times higher than the geometric mean across the subsequent 10 years (2001-2010), representing an 18 percent decrease between 1999-2000 and 2001-2010. For blood MeHg, the geometric mean in 1999-2000 was 1.51 times higher than the geometric mean across the subsequent 10 years. This represents a decrease of 34 percent between 1999-2000 and 2001-2010. The linear time trend in the means of the log-transformed data is not statistically significant for THg at the 5 percent level (p=0.11), but it is for MeHg (p=0.0006). However, when survey release 1999-2000 is excluded from the analysis, there is no statistically significant time trend for MeHg (p=0.74) from 2001-2002 to 2009-2010. There is a statistically significant linear tend in the percent above the overall 90th percentile for both THg (p=0.004) and MeHg (p=0.003). Excluding survey release 1999-2000 from the analysis, there is no statistically significant trend in the percent above the overall 90th percentile for either THg (p=0.72) of MeHg (p=0.58).

The percentage of participants with blood THg and blood MeHg over 5.8 µg/L in each of the survey releases are shown in Table 5. The percentage of women of reproductive age with blood THg over 5.8 µg/L in 1999-2000 was 2.64 times that found in 2001-2010, a decrease of 62 percent between 1999-2000 and 2001-2010. For blood MeHg, the percent of women of reproductive age over 5.8 µg/L in 1999-2000 was 2.86 times higher than the percent of women in 2001-2010, representing a 65 percent decrease between 1999-2000 and 2001-2010. There are significant differences between the survey releases for both THg and MeHg (chi-square p-value <.0001), with 1999-2000 having approximately twice the number of women with levels over 5.8 µg/L compared to the other sets of years. Excluding survey release 1999-2000 from the analysis, there are no significant differences between the survey releases for either THg (chi-square p-value = 0.57) or MeHg (chi-square p-value = 0.56).

Table 5.   **Percent of women aged 16 to 49 years with blood MeHg > 5.8 µg/L, by NHANES survey release**

Survey Release	Percent THg >5.8 µg/L (SE)	Percent MeHg >5.8 µg/L (SE)
Overall	*3.45 (0.36)*	*3.14 (0.34)*
1999-2000	7.13 (1.78)	6.77 (1.77)
2001-2002	3.67 (0.72)	3.14 (0.71)
2003-2004	2.40 (0.82)	1.70 (0.70)
2005-2006	2.67 (0.60)	2.33 (0.58)
2007-2008	2.49 (0.60)	2.42 (0.56)
2009-2010	2.30 (0.41)	2.14 (0.36)

More detailed tabulations of the blood mercury distributions, including sample sizes and 25th, 50th, 75th, 90th, and 95th percentiles, are in the Appendix, Tables A-2 and A-3. Table A-2 shows the distributions of blood THg and Table A-3 shows the distributions for blood MeHg for all women aged 16-49, by NHANES survey release, by race/ethnicity, by income, and by age.

3.2   Trends in Fish consumption

3.2.1   Trends in Frequency of Consumption

Figure 3 displays the percent of women aged 16-49 years in each of six categories of reported 30-day fish frequency consumption. Detailed tabulations are in the Appendix, Table A-4. Note that the percentages for consuming finfish only or shellfish only zero times in the past 30 days are greater than the percent consuming total finfish/shellfish zero times in the past 30 days because some participants only consume finfish or only consume shellfish. And the percent consuming total finfish/shellfish six or more times in the past 30 days is greater than for either finfish or shellfish alone as individuals who consumed shellfish less than 6 times and finfish less than 6 times can have a total greater than 6 when combined. While there are statistically significant differences in consumption frequency between the survey releases (Rao-Scott Chi-Square p-values: p=0.03 for total fish, p=0.02 for finfish, p=0.16 for shellfish), there is not a consistent trend over time. Approximately 8 percent more women reported consuming fish 6 times or more in the previous 30 days in 2005-2006 (34.2%) compared to 1999-2000 (26.4%). The percentage of women reporting this frequency of consumption in 2007-2008 (26.9%) drops back to what was observed in 1999-2000 data then increases again in 2009-2010 (31.8%).

Figure 3.   **Percent of participants by 30-day fish consumption frequency, by NHANES survey release, women aged 16-49 years**

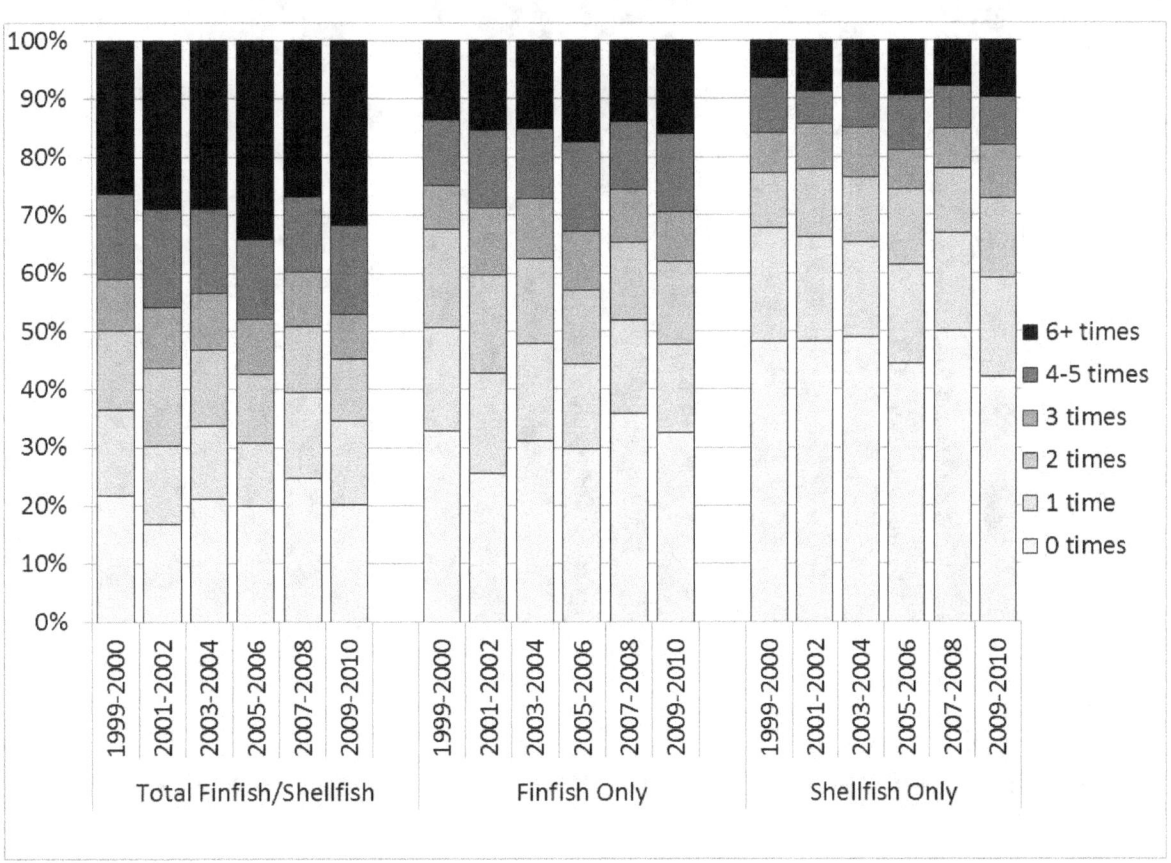

Figure 4 summarizes the frequency of consumption by demographics of interest: income, race/ethnicity, and age. The figure shows differences in frequency of fish consumption between income group, race/ethnicity, and age (all have Rao-Scott Chi-Square p-values <.0001). Higher income is associated with increased frequency of fish consumption as is older age. Women in the "Other Race" category, which includes Asian, Pacific Islander, American Indian, Alaska Native, multi-racial, eat fish more frequently than Hispanic, non-Hispanic white, and non-Hispanic black women. These findings agree with previous literature (Kudo et al., 2000; Sechena et al., 2003; Mahaffey et al., 2004). Since these demographic characteristics are associated with fish consumption, they were included in the multivariate analyses discussed in Section 3.4.

Figure 4. Percent of participants by 30-day fish consumption frequency, by demographic characteristics, women aged 16-49 years, NHANES 1999-2008

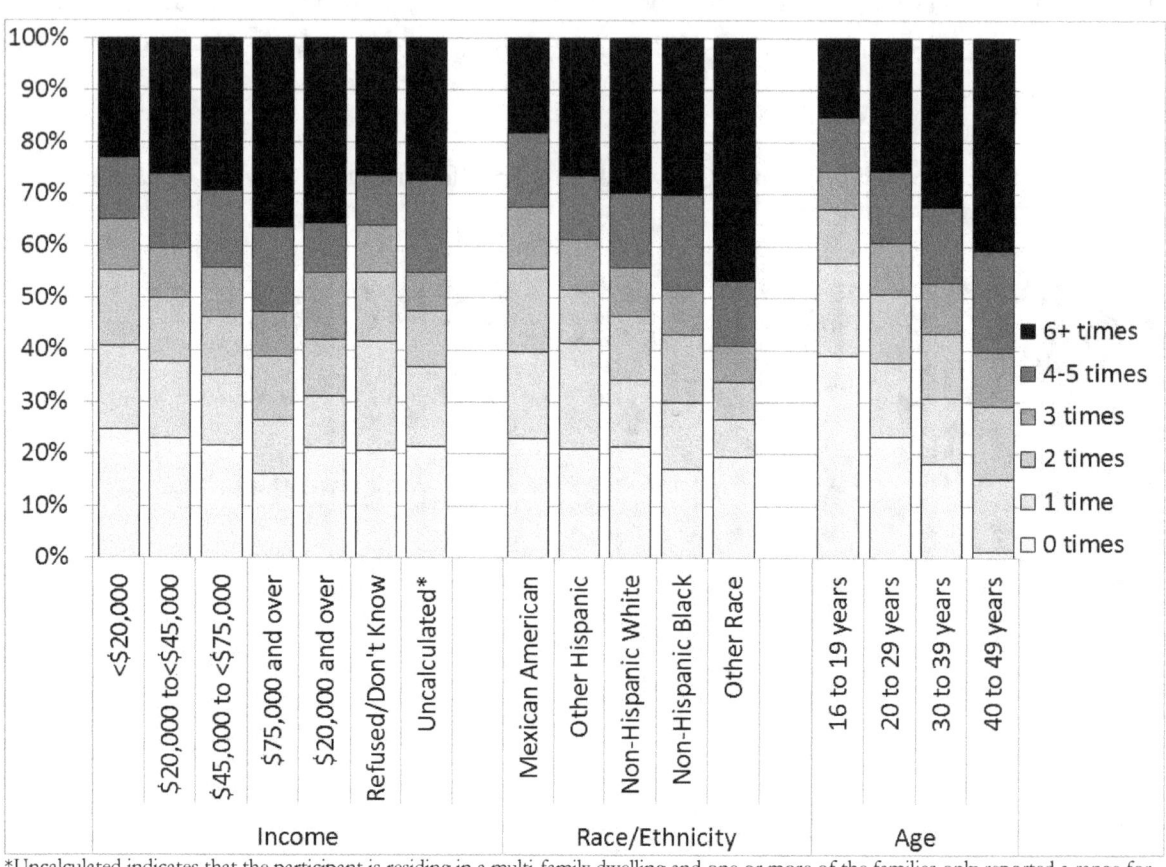

*Uncalculated indicates that the participant is residing in a multi-family dwelling and one or more of the families only reported a range for their family income, either <$20,000 or >$20,000. Thus NCHS did not calculate household income for these participants.

3.2.2   Trends in Estimated Amounts Consumed Over the Previous 30 Days

Detailed tables on the amounts of fish consumed are in the Appendix, Tables A-5 through A-8. Tables A-5, A-6, and A-7 present estimates of amounts of fish eaten (g), mercury intake (µg), and mercury intake per unit body weight (µg/kg) over the previous 30 days, by NHANES survey release. Table A-8 presents the same statistics by income, race/ethnicity, and age. The estimates are presented for shellfish consumption, finfish consumption, and combined fish/shellfish consumption. The presented statistics include number of sampled women age 16-49, arithmetic means and their 95% confidence intervals, 25th, 50th, 75th, 90th, and 95th percentiles and their 95%

confidence intervals. Presented here are summaries from Tables A-5 and A-6.

Figure 5 displays the estimated mean amounts of fish consumed over a 30-day period by women aged 16-49 and the 90th percentiles. There is no evidence of a trend over time in the consumption of fish in either the mean (p=0.31) or the percent over the overall 90th percentile (p=0.30).

Figure 5. **Estimated mean and 90th percentile amounts of fish consumed in 30 days, women aged 16-49 years, NHANES 1999-2010 (with 95% confidence intervals)**

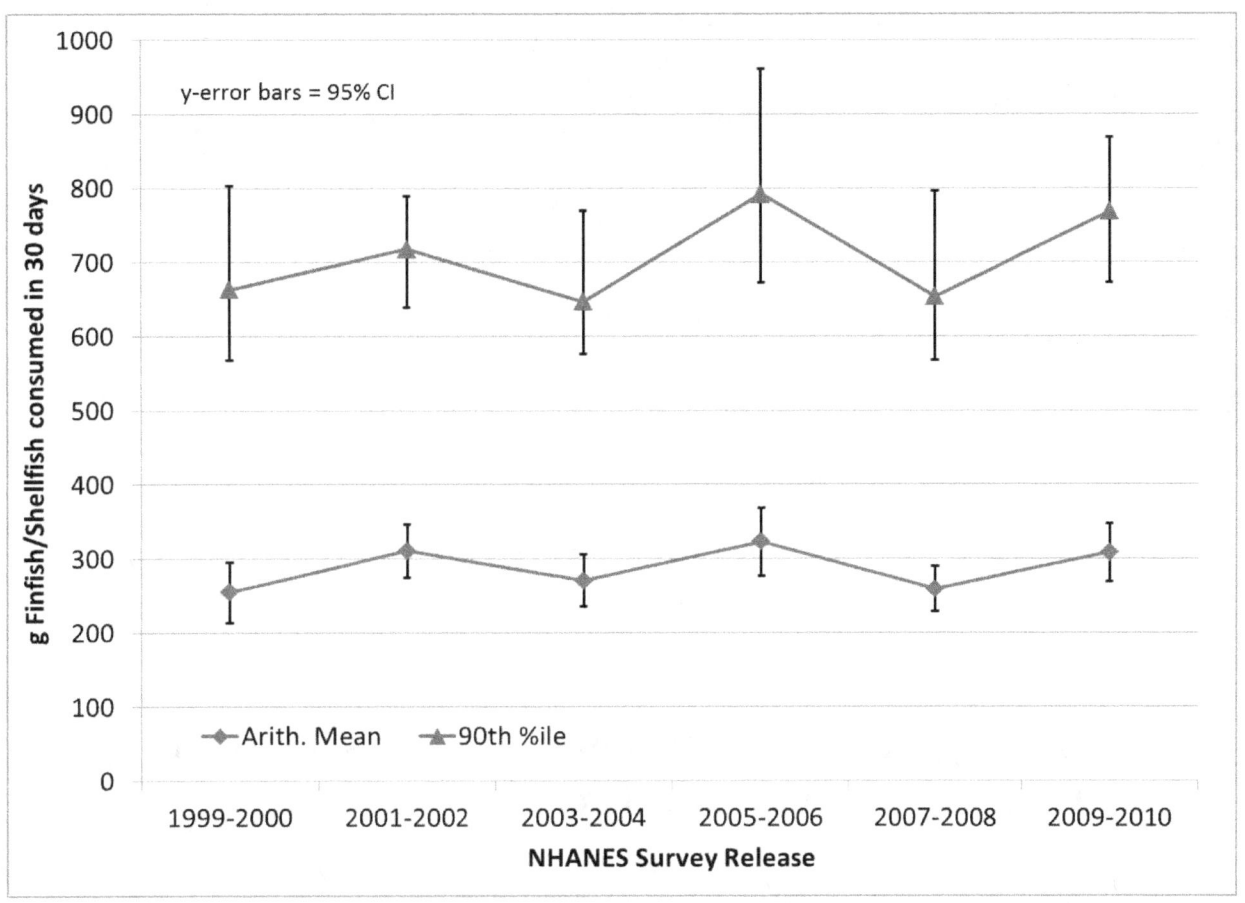

Figure 6 displays the estimated mean amounts of mercury ingested by eating fish per unit body weight. The patterns over time are different than those observed in Figure 5 for estimated 30-day fish consumed. At both the mean and the 90th percentile there appears to be a decrease over time in μg mercury ingested per kg body weight. However, this change is not statistically significant (p=0.35 for the mean and p=0.92 for the percent over the overall 90th percentile). The different patterns observed in figures 5 and 6 indicate that women who are the highest fish consumers are possibly shifting to lower mercury fish.

Figure 6. Estimated mean and 90th percentile amounts of mercury ingested, normed to body weight (µg/kg) in 30 days, women aged 16-49 years, NHANES 1999-2010 (with 95% confidence intervals)

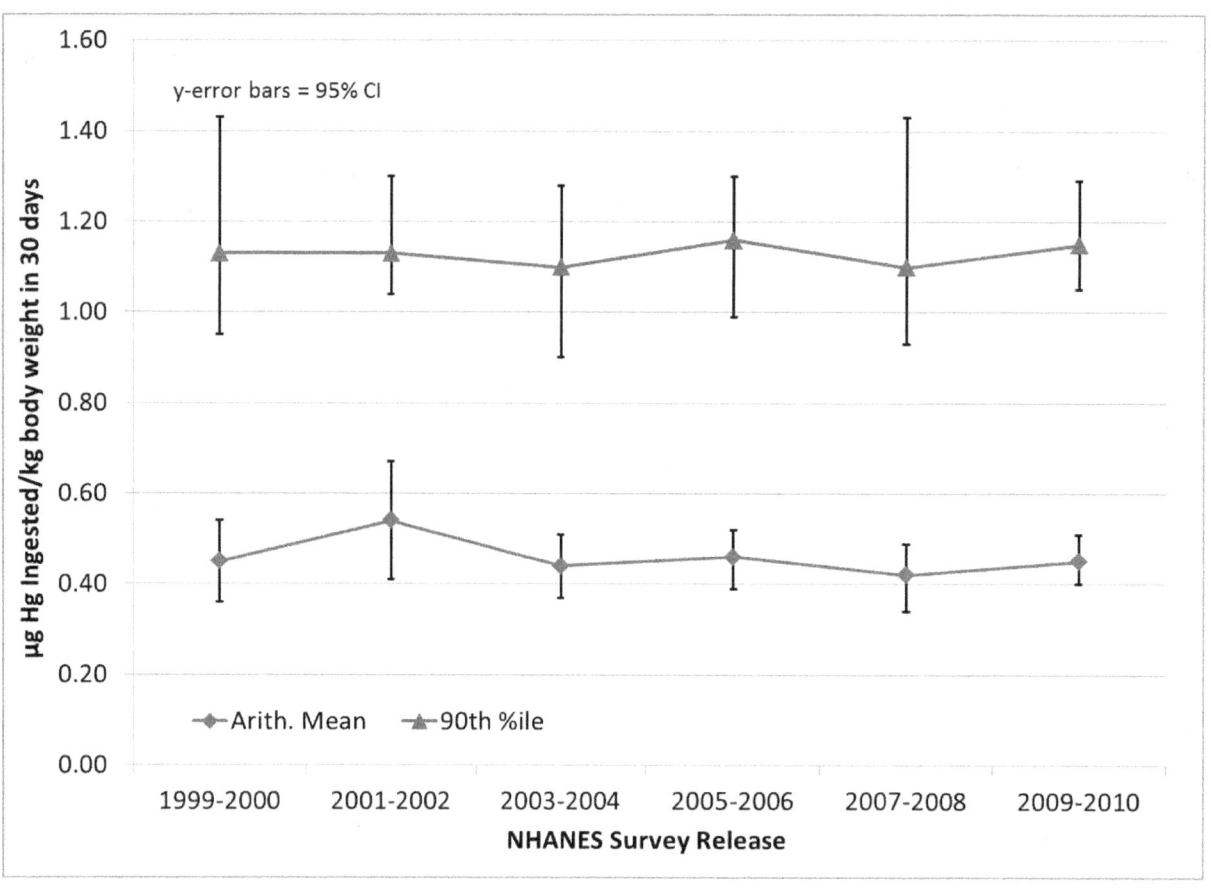

3.3 Associations between Fish Consumption Frequency and Blood Mercury Concentrations

This section examines statistical associations between fish consumption and blood mercury concentrations, especially with respect to changes over time.

Figures 7 and 8 display the concentration of blood THg and blood MeHg by frequency of fish consumption in 30 days, using box plots. As expected, both blood THg ($p<.0001$) and blood MeHg ($p=0.003$) increase with frequency of fish consumption. These figures agree with previous findings (Schober et al., 2003; Mahaffey et al., 2004; Mahaffey et al., 2009) that people who eat fish more frequently tend to have higher blood mercury levels and, further, there is a dose-response gradient observed in the mean.

Figure 7. Distribution of blood THg (µg/L), by reported frequency of fish consumption in 30 days, women aged 16-49 years, NHANES 1999-2010

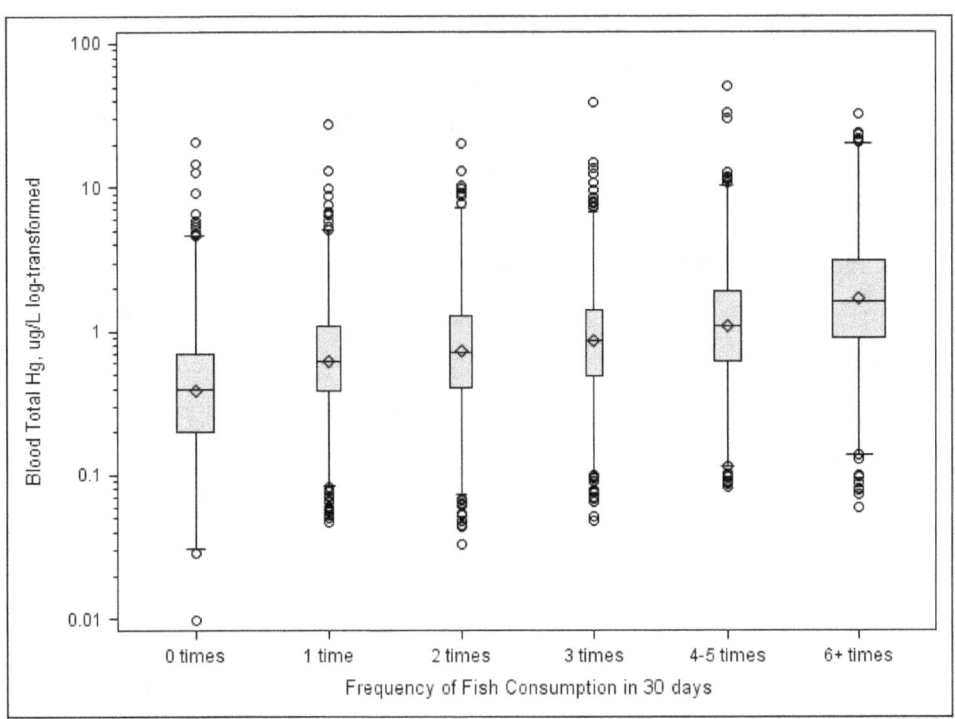

Figure 8. Distribution of blood MeHg (µg/L), by reported frequency of fish consumption in 30 days, women aged 16-49 years, NHANES 1999-2010

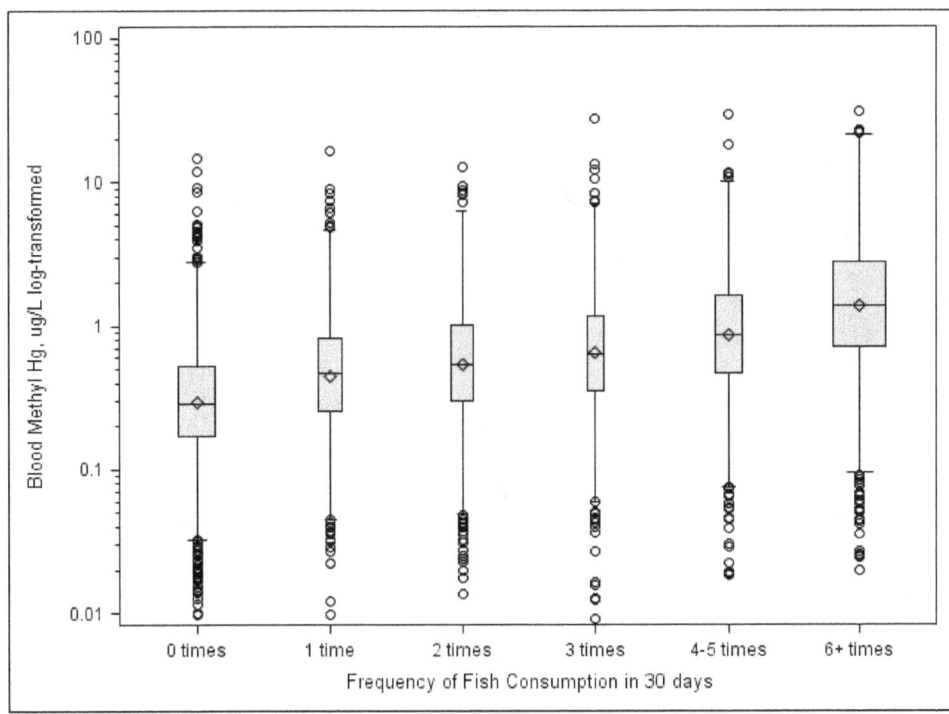

Figure 9 displays mean blood MeHg levels against the reported 30-day frequency of consumption of fish, for each of the six two-year periods. Detailed tables are in the Appendix, Table A-9. This figure also shows a statistically significant change over time. Women who ate fish more frequently in 2009-2010 had lower blood MeHg levels than women who ate fish with the same frequency in 1999-2000. For example, among women who ate fish 6 or more times, the arithmetic mean blood mercury level was 3.36 (2.75,3.97) µg/L in 1999-2000; in 2009-2010, it had dropped to 2.11 (1.87,2.35) µg/L, a statistically significant decrease. However, the lowest concentrations are observed in survey release 2005-2006, with an arithmetic mean of 1.84 (1.61,2.08) µg/L, with slight increase the two following survey periods. Similarly, the 90th percentile of blood MeHg dropped from 8.33 (6.28,11.07) µg/L to 4.24 (3.54,5.08) µg/L. These findings suggest that women who consume fish more often may be shifting to fish with lower concentrations of mercury.

Figure 9. Mean blood MeHg concentrations by reported frequency of fish consumption in 30 days, women aged 16-49 years, NHANES 1999-2010 (with 95% confidence intervals, median, and 90th percentile)

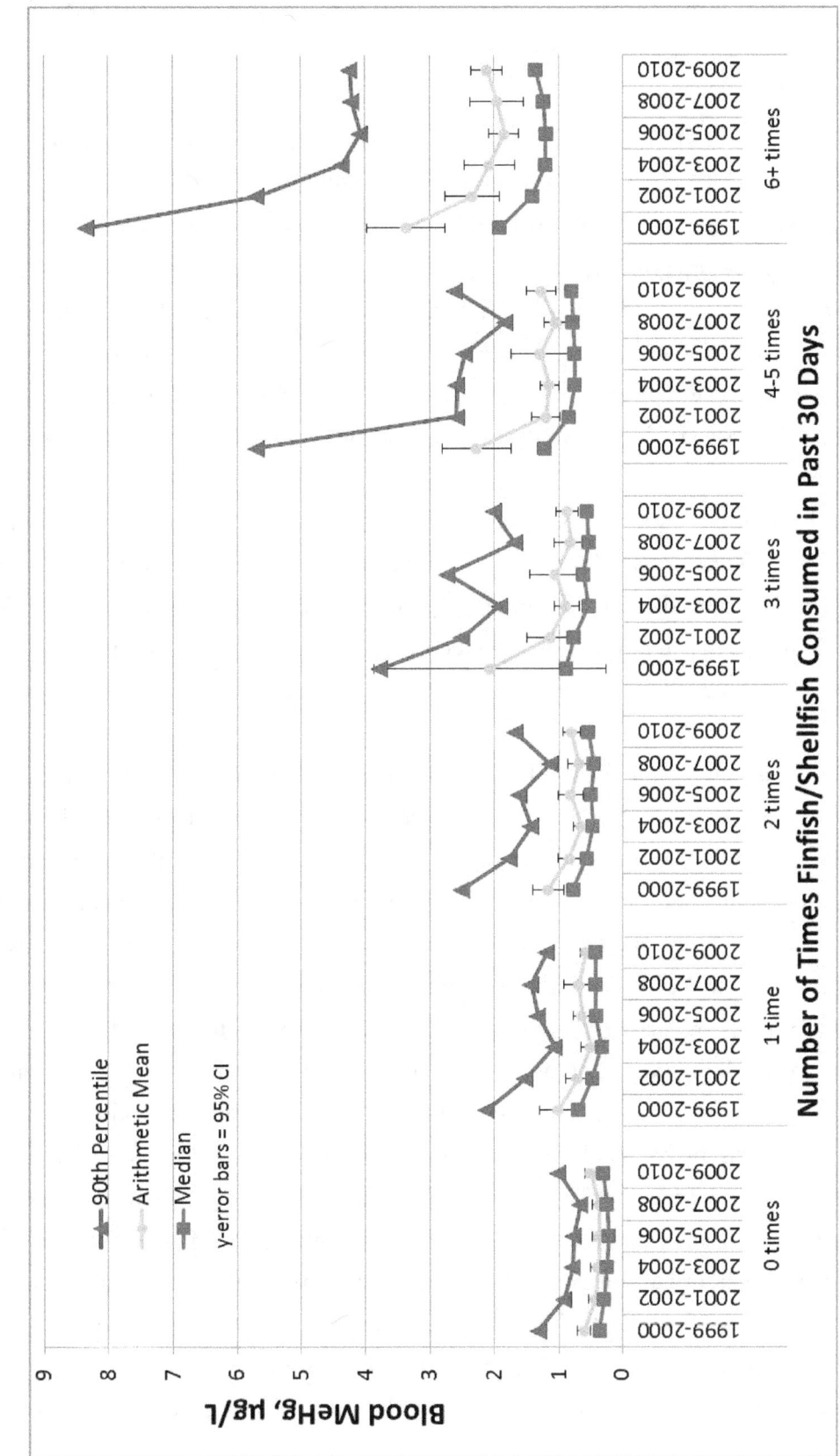

29

3.4   Regression Analysis Results: Associations between Blood Mercury, Fish Consumption, Time, and Demographic Factors

To better understand the relationship between blood MeHg concentration and time, adjusting for factors known to be associated with fish consumption, a nonlinear model was fit to predict the log transformed MeHg concentration from transformed mercury intake and demographic characteristics. The model assumed that there was a linear relationship between blood MeHg concentration and mercury intake from fish. Predicting the log-transformed blood MeHg has the advantages that the prediction errors have relatively constant variance, as assumed by the model, and the predicted values are always positive. Using the non-linear model has the advantage that the intercept and slope for mercury intake have the same interpretation as when using linear models.

Table 6 shows the parameter estimates, standard errors, p-values, and relative ratios from the nonlinear model. The intercept and slope are equivalent to the intercept and slope in a linear model predicting blood MeHg from fish mercury intake. The other demographic parameters model multiplicative differences in the blood MeHg concentrations. Multiplicative differences corresponding to the parameters are in the Relative Ratio column.

The slope parameter is highly significant, indicating an increase in blood MeHg with an increase in mercury intake per body weight (p < 0.0001). MeHg concentrations also depend on the participant's income (p < 0.0001), age (p < 0.0001), and race (p < 0.0001). Blood MeHg concentrations increase with increasing age; however, at older ages the increase diminishes. Blood MeHg concentrations increase with increasing income such that those with household income above $75,000 have MeHg concentrations about 1.5 times higher than those with income less than $20,000. However, interpreting the trend is complicated by how the income data are reported. Blood MeHg concentrations also vary by race category with non-Hispanic whites and Mexican Americans having lower concentrations than non-Hispanic blacks and other Hispanics and races other than those listed (other races) having the highest levels. The blood MeHg concentrations for other races are about 1.8 times higher than for non-Hispanic whites. Differences among NHANES survey releases are also statistically significant (p < 0.0001). Blood MeHg concentrations from survey release 1999-2000 are significantly higher than the mean of the other years (p<.0001). The linear trend after 1999-2000 is not statistically significant (p=0.72), but the quadratic trend after 1999-2000 is (p=0.004). This corresponds to decreasing blood MeHg concentrations followed by relatively small changes and a slight increase in the last years. When extrapolated backward, the quadratic trend fit to the data after 2000 and the geometric mean from the first NHANES survey release, 1999-2000, are not significantly different (p=0.34).

Table 6. Parameter estimates and relative ratios from the non-linear model predicting blood MeHg concentrations

	Parameter	Std. Error	p-Value	Relative Ratio
Intercept	0.44	0.07	0.0076	
Hg/Wt Slope	1.05	0.08	<0.0001	
Body Weight	-0.09	0.05	0.08	
Age, Overall			<0.0001	
Age	0.34	0.05	<0.0001	
Age2	-0.28	0.13	0.04	
Income, Overall			<0.0001	
0 to 20K	-0.16	0.04	<0.0001	0.85
20 to 45K	-0.07	0.03	0.04	0.93
45 to 75K	0.00	0.03	0.97	1.00
>75K	0.25	0.04	<0.0001	1.29
MultiHH	-0.01	0.07	0.90	0.99
Refuse/DK	0.07	0.09	0.42	1.08
Over 20K	-0.09	0.08	0.29	0.92
Race, Overall			<0.0001	
Non-Hispanic Black	0.14	0.04	0.0012	1.15
Mexican Amer.	-0.27	0.04	<0.0001	0.76
Other Hispanic	0.04	0.05	0.45	1.04
Other Race	0.33	0.05	<0.0001	1.39
Non-Hispanic White	-0.24	0.04	<0.0001	0.79
NHANES Year, Overall			<0.0001	
1999-2000 different from post-2000 mean	0.47	0.09	<0.0001	
Linear trend after 1999-2000	-0.005	0.01	0.71	
Quadratic trend after 1999-2000	0.05	0.02	0.0038	
1999-2000 diff. from post-2000 quadratic trend	0.11	0.11	0.35	

The same model described above was fit for blood THg. The results were similar for all independent variables except for the year terms. When extrapolated backward, the quadratic trend fit to the data after 2000 corresponds to a significantly lower THg concentration for the first NHANES survey release, 1999-2000, than observed (p=0.004).

The non-linear model predicts the mean of the log-transformed blood MeHg concentrations. However, the upper percentiles may follow a somewhat different pattern. To test if there is a trend in the upper percentiles, logistic regression was used to model the probability of a blood MeHg measurement over 5.8 μg/L. Overall 3.1% of concentrations are greater than 5.8 μg/L. The predictors in the model include scaled age (as a linear and quadratic parameter), dummy variables for income and race, quadratic trends across NHANES survey release (including the difference between the 1999-200 release and later releases), and transformed fish mercury intake. The model used the transformation of fish mercury intake derived from the non-linear model. The parameter estimates shown in the equation below, are the parameter estimates from the nonlinear model (Table 6.).

$$Transformed(HgIntake) = ln(0.4388 + 1.0492HgIntake)$$

Table 7 shows the parameter estimates, standard errors, odds ratios, and p-values from the logistic regression model. Differences among NHANES survey releases are statistically significant ($p<.0001$). The probability of having blood mercury concentration greater than 5.8 μg/L is higher in 1999-2000 survey release ($p<.0001$). Neither the linear nor quadratic trend since 1999-2000 is statistically significant at the 5 percent level. The probability of MeHg concentrations over 5.8 μg/L also depends on the participant's income ($p<.0001$), age ($p = 0.002$), and race/ethnicity ($p <.0001$). The probability generally increases with increasing age. Probabilities increase with increasing income. However, interpreting the trend is complicated by how the income data are reported. Probabilities also vary by race/ethnicity category with lower probabilities for Mexican Americans and higher probabilities for the "Other race" category.

Table 7. Parameter estimates and odds ratios from the logistic model predicting the probability of blood MeHg concentrations over 5.8 µg/L

	Parameter	Std. Error	p-Value	Odds Ratio
Intercept	-3.80	0.23	<0.0001	
Transformed Mercury Intake	1.42	0.13	<0.0001	
Body Weight	-0.61	0.35	0.09	
Age, Overall			0.0018	
Age	0.92	0.31	0.0035	
Age^2	-1.91	0.98	0.06	
Income, Overall			<0.0001	
0 to 20K	-0.99	0.33	0.0037	0.37
20 to 45K	0.0007	0.21	1.00	1.00
45 to 75K	0.04	0.25	0.87	1.04
>75K	0.56	0.21	0.0095	1.75
MultiHH	-0.20	0.35	0.56	0.82
Refuse/DK	0.67	0.49	0.17	1.96
Over 20K	-0.09	0.61	0.89	0.92
Race, Overall			<0.0001	
Non-Hispanic Black	0.37	0.14	0.0116	1.45
Mexican Amer.	-1.39	0.24	<0.0001	0.25
Other Hispanic	-0.33	0.49	0.50	0.72
Other Race	1.34	0.24	<0.0001	3.82
Non-Hispanic White	0.01	0.22	0.97	1.01
NHANES Year, Overall			<0.0001	
1999-2000 different from others	1.43	0.29	<0.0001	
Linear trend after 1999-2000	-0.09	0.07	0.25	
Quadratic trend after 1999-2000	0.05	0.07	0.45	
1999-2000 diff. from quadratic trend	0.81	0.60	0.18	

3.5 Regression Analysis Results: Associations between Fish Consumption and Intake of Mercury with Time and Demographic Factors

To better understand the relationship between fish consumption and time, logistic regression was used to model the probability of a person reporting any fish consumption in the previous 30 days, and for those with fish consumption, five regression models were fit to predict fish consumption and mercury intake variables from demographic characteristics and NHANES survey release. These variables were amount of fish consumed in a meal (meal size), number of meals in 30 days, the mercury concentration in the fish consumed (calculated as the ratio of 30-day mercury intake to 30-day fish consumption), the inverse of body weight, and the mercury intake per unit body weight. Full model results to assess a linear time trend in each of these components are presented in the appendix (Tables A-10 to A-15). The results from the models treating all predictors as categorical (to facilitate presentation) are summarized in Figures 10 through 14.

Figure 10 presents the results from the regression models for the race/ethnicity categories. The parenthetical percentages beside the race/ethnicity group, e.g., white, non-Hispanic (65%), are the percent of the total study population that comprises that category. The grey filled star symbols and error bars plotted on the second y-axis are the percent of that category that reported any fish consumption in the previous 30 days. The remaining colored symbols and error bars are, for fish consumers, the relative ratios (RR) and 95 percent confidence intervals from the regression models predicting 1) the log-transformed frequency of fish consumption in the previous 30 days (red open diamond symbol); 2) the log-transformed meal size (green filled circle symbol); 3) the log-transformed mercury concentration in the fish consumed (orange filled diamond symbol); 4) the log-transformed inverse of body weight (blue open circle symbol); and 5) the log-transformed mercury intake per unit body weight (black filled square symbol). The horizontal line on the plot at RR = 1 represents the geometric mean response for a hypothetical population equally divided among categories for race or other categorical variables. This will be referred to as the response for a typical participant. If a symbol is above the line at RR = 1, then that racial/ethnic group is higher than the geometric mean for a typical participant for that fish consumption or mercury intake variable. For example, non-Hispanic white women consume fish with higher geometric mean mercury concentrations than the typical women (orange filled diamond symbol). Correspondingly, if a symbol is below the line at RR = 1, then that racial/ethnic group is lower than typical for that variable. For example, Mexican American women reported fewer meals in 30 days (red open diamond symbol) compared to the geometric mean for a typical participant. The blue open circle symbol is the relative ratio of the *inverse* of body weight, thus a RR greater than one indicates lower body weight than typical and a RR less than one indicates higher body weight than typical.

Figure 10. Relative ratios and 95% confidence limits from the models predicting fish consumption and mercury intake variables versus race/ethnicity

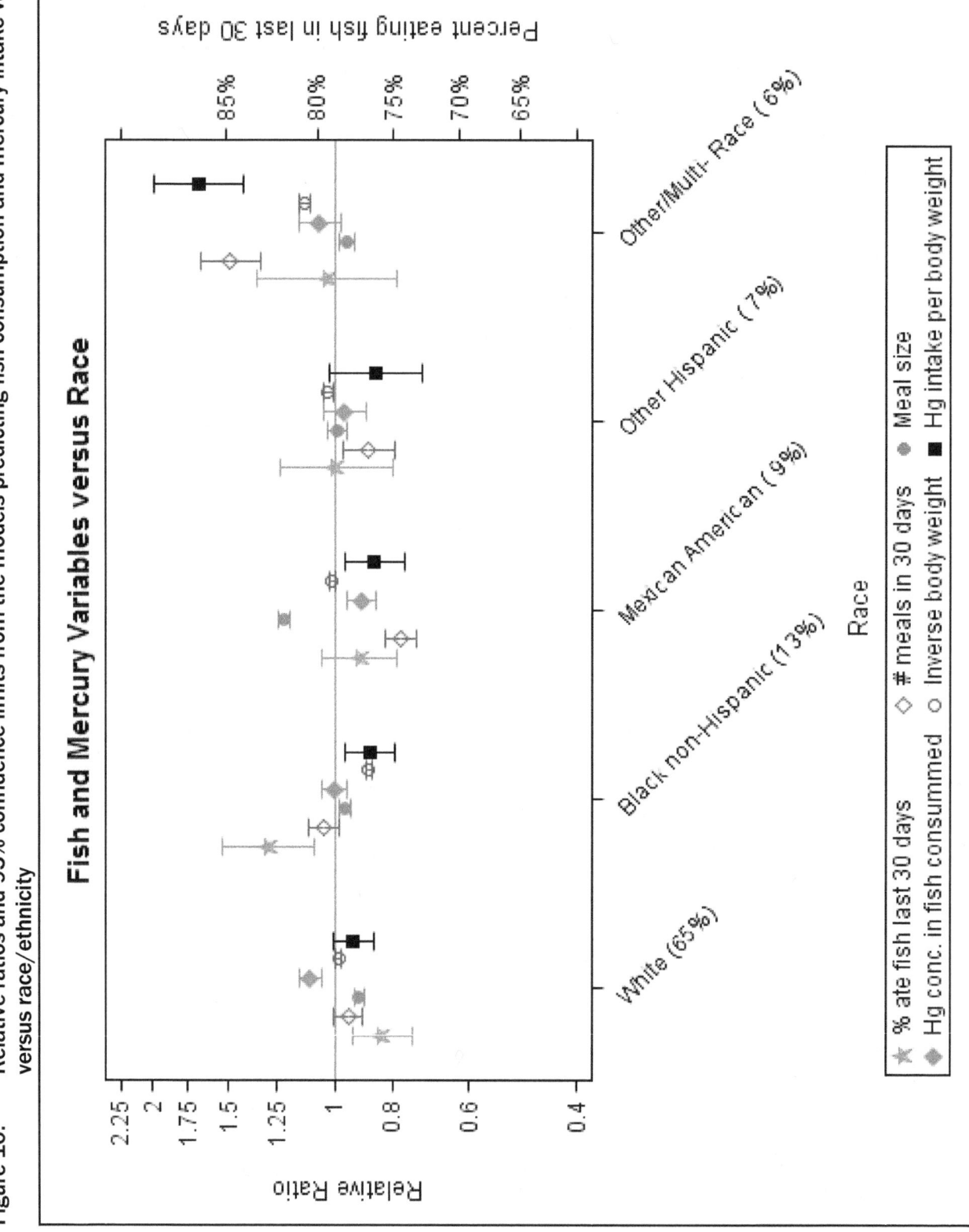

The distance of the RR from the reference line of one, for a particular racial/ethnic group (e.g., other Hispanic), can be summed across four of the models (meal size, number of meals in 30 days, the mercury concentration in the fish consumed, and the inverse of body weight) to approximately equal the distance from one of the RR of the fifth model, mercury intake per kg body weight. Figure 11 presents an extract of the full plot displayed in Figure 10 to illustrate this point.

As seen in both Figure 10 and Figure 11, other Hispanics consume fish less frequently, their meal sizes are smaller, the mercury concentration in the fish consumed is less, and their body weights are less than typical. In Figure 11, the brackets to the right of each symbol show the distance of the RR from one. These distances can be combined to equal the RR for the fifth model, mercury intake per unit body weight, as shown by the brackets to the right of the black filled square symbol. Note that the RR for the inverse of body weight is the only one for other Hispanics that is above one, thus it is subtracted from the total of the other distances. For the race category, other/multi-race, all RRs except for meal size are greater than one, thus the distances from the other three models are summed and the distance from the model of meal size is subtracted, to equal the distance of the RR of the fifth model.

There are statistically significant differences for all of the fish consumption and mercury intake variables by race/ethnicity. The p-values testing the overall significance of race/ethnicity in all models is $p < .0001$. The proportion of non-Hispanic black women who consumed fish in the previous 30 days is higher than for other racial/ethnic categories while the proportion of non-Hispanic white women is less (Figure 10). Other/Multi-race women consume fish the most frequently, consume fish with higher concentrations of mercury, and have lower body weights, resulting in the highest mercury intake per unit body weight of the racial/ethnic categories. Mexican American women consume the largest meal sizes; however they eat fish less frequently compared to the other racial/ethnic groups, resulting in low mercury intake per unit body weight. Non-Hispanic black women consume larger meal sizes than typical; however, their body weights are greater than typical, resulting in lower than typical mercury intake per unit body weight. Non-Hispanic white women consume fish with higher concentration of mercury than typical; however they consume fish less frequently than typical and have smaller meal sizes, resulting in a lower than typical mercury intake per unit body weight.

Figure 11. Extract of the full plot of fish and mercury variables versus race/ethnicity

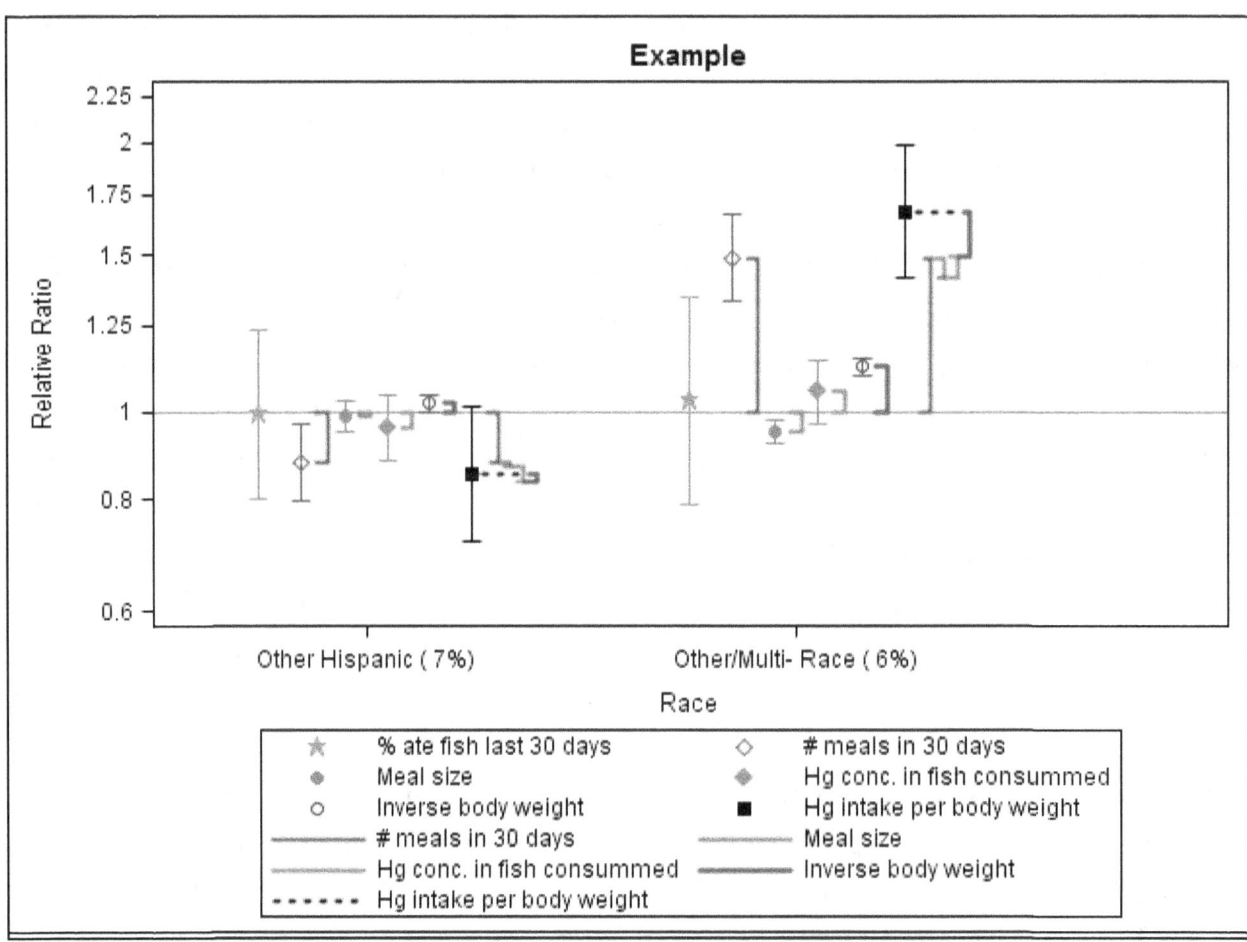

Figure 12 displays the RRs of age groups for each of the fish consumption and mercury intake variables. The p-values testing the overall significance of age in all models is p<.0001, except for the model of mercury concentration of the fish consumed which has a p-value of 0.0002. The percent of women who consumed fish in the previous 30 days increases with increasing age. All of the factors that contribute to mercury intake per unit body weight increase with increasing age. Women aged 16 to 19 years have the lowest intakes of mercury per unit body weight: they consume fish less frequently, eat smaller meal sizes, consume fish with low concentrations of mercury, and have the lowest body weights of all age groups. Women aged 40 to 49 years have the highest intakes of mercury per unit body weight: they consume fish most frequently, eat the largest meal sizes, consume fish with higher concentrations of mercury, and have the highest body weights of all age groups.

Figure 13 displays the RRs of income groups for each of the fish consumption and mercury intake variables. The p-values testing the overall significance of income in the models are as follows; for the proportion that consumed fish in the previous 30 days, p<.0001; for the frequency of fish consumption in the previous 30 days, p<.0001; for the meal size, p=0.44; for mercury concentration of the fish consumed, p=0.13, for body weight, p<.0001, and for mercury intake per unit body weight, p<.0001. Due to how income data were collected, it is difficult to fully assess trends across income level. However, mercury intake per unit body weight is highest in the income categories $75K and up and $20k and up. In both cases, the frequency of fish consumed in 30 days, the meal size, and the mercury concentration in the fish consumed are higher than other income groups. Additionally, body weight decreases with increasing income. All of these factors contribute to the increased mercury intake per unit body weight in the higher income groups.

Figure 14 displays the RRs of NHANES survey release for each of the fish consumption and mercury intake variables. The p-values testing for a trend across time in the models are as follows; for the proportion that consumed fish in the previous 30 days, p=0.21; for the frequency of fish consumption in the previous 30 days, p=0.37; for the meal size, p=0.46; for mercury concentration of the fish consumed, p=0.035; for body weight, p=0.20; and for mercury intake per unit body weight, p=0.35. Women from NHANES 2001-2002 and 2005-2006 have the highest mercury intake per unit body weight. In NHANES 2001-2002, women consumed fish with higher concentrations of mercury and had larger than typical meal sizes. In NHANES 2005-2006, women consumed fish more frequently than typical. NHANES 2007-2008 has the lowest mercury intake per unit body weight. Women in this survey period ate fish with low mercury concentrations and consumed fish the least frequently. The decreasing trend in mercury concentration in the fish consumed (the ratio of mercury intake to fish consumed) is consistent with women shifting consumption to species with lower concentrations of mercury over time.

Figure 12. Relative ratios and 95% confidence limits from the models predicting fish consumption and mercury intake variables versus age

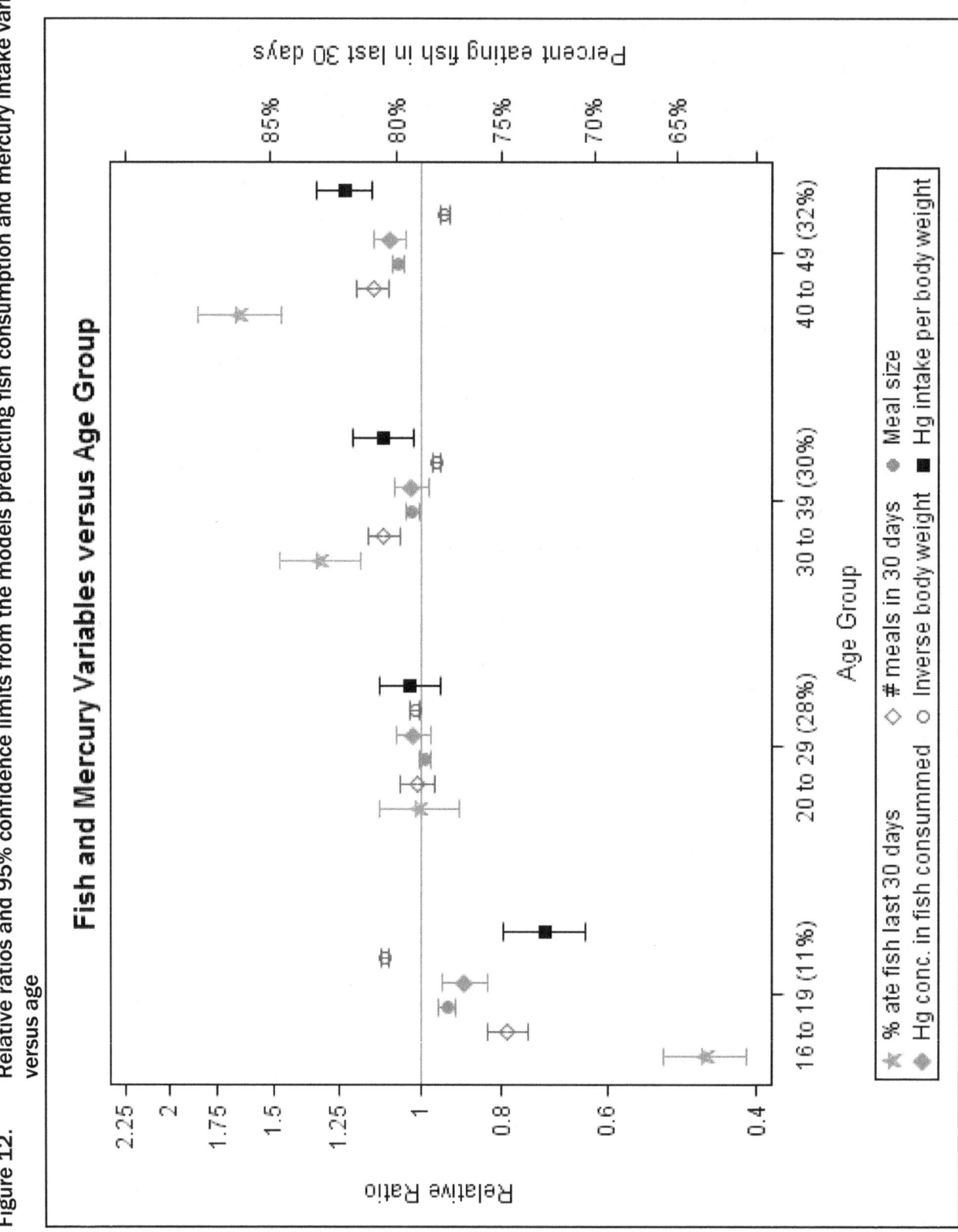

Figure 13.   Relative ratios and 95% confidence limits from the models predicting fish consumption and mercury intake variables versus income

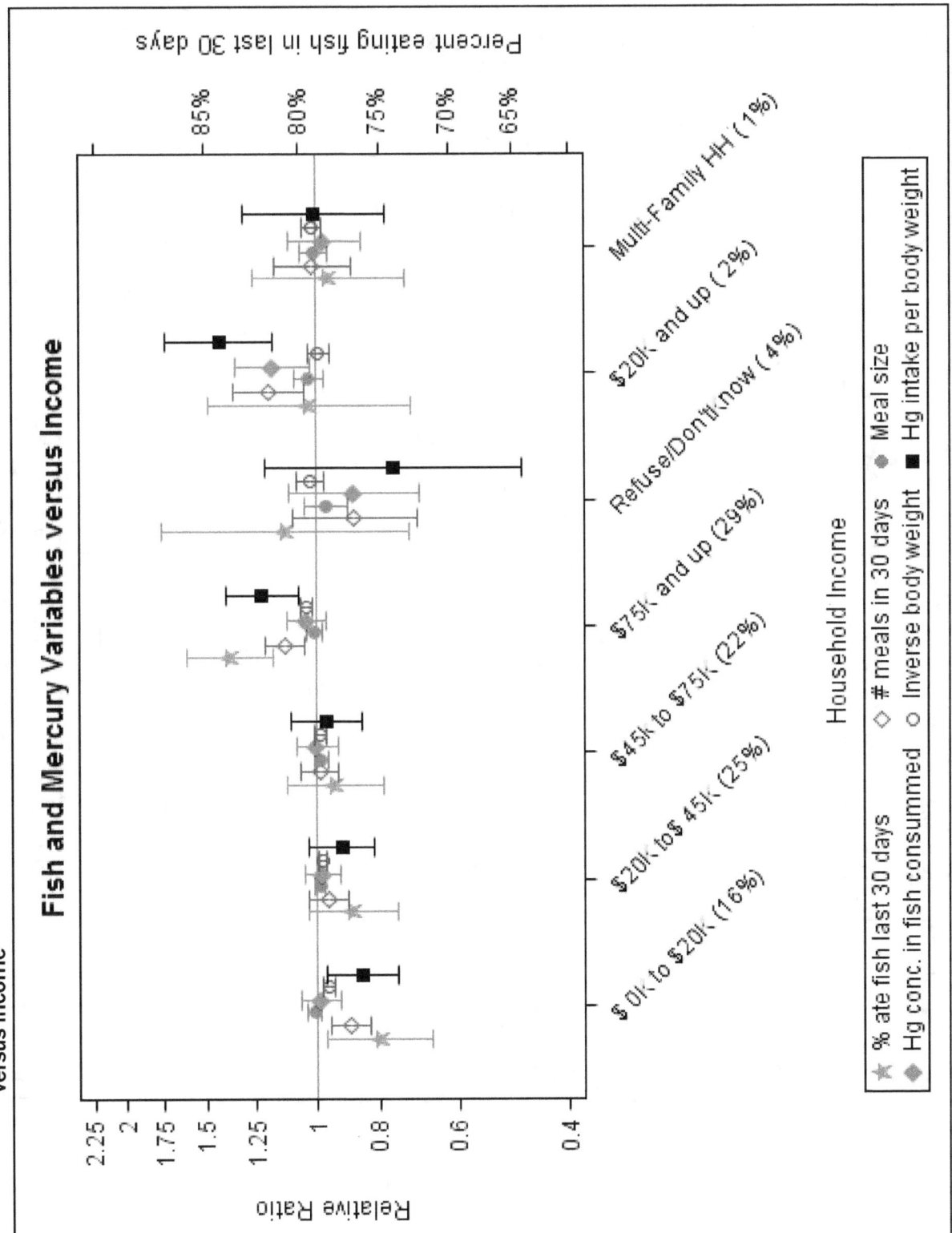

Figure 14. Relative ratios and 95% confidence limits from the models predicting fish consumption and mercury intake variables versus NHANES survey release

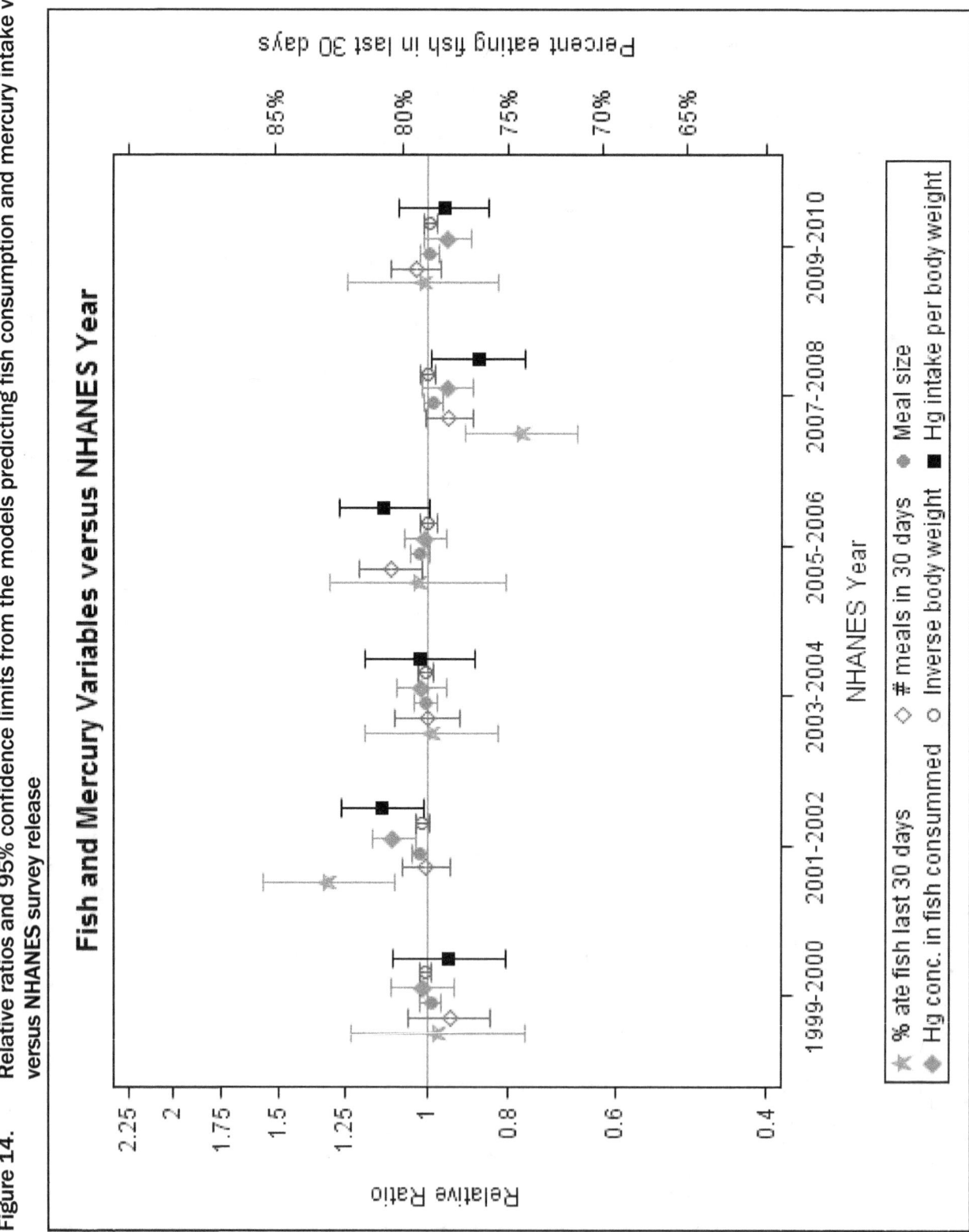

Discussion **4**

This analysis found statistically significant differences in blood MeHg and blood THg concentrations across the study period in both the mean concentrations and the upper percentiles. The nonlinear model predicting the log-transformed blood MeHg found survey release 1999-2000 to be significantly higher than the mean of the other releases ($p<.0001$) and a significant quadratic trend ($p=0.004$) from 2001-2002 to 2009-2010, indicating decreasing blood MeHg concentrations, followed by relatively small changes and a slight increase in the last years. The nonlinear model predicting the log-transformed blood THg found NHANES survey release 1999-2000 to be significantly higher than the mean of the other sets of NHANES survey releases ($p=0.0005$) and no statistically significant trend since 2000. The logistic model predicting the probability of MeHg >5.8 $\mu g/L$ found that women from survey release 1999-2000 had higher probability of having blood MeHg >5.8 $\mu g/L$ ($p<.0001$) and no statistically significant trend since 2000. Demographic characteristics found to be associated with blood mercury in other studies (Schober et al., 2003; Mahaffey et al., 2004; Mahaffey et al., 2009; Caldwell et al., 2009) showed the same relationships in this analysis. There was a significant relationship between mercury intake from fish consumption and blood mercury ($p<.0001$) in all three models. However, after adjusting for mercury intake, there were additional differences in blood mercury between the survey releases.

The analysis showed few changes in fish consumption and mercury intake over the study period. Chi-square analysis found a statistically significant difference in the reported frequency of consumption ($p=0.03$) across survey releases; however, the model predicting the frequency of consumption among consumers found no significant trend over time. It did find significant relationships between race, age, and income with frequency of consumption ($p<.0001$). There was no evidence of a trend in either estimated 30-day fish consumption or mercury intake per unit body weight. There was a marginally statistically significant decreasing trend across the NHANES survey releases in the ratio of mercury intake to fish consumed ($p=0.035$) that is consistent with women shifting their consumption to fish with lower mercury concentrations. The decrease observed in blood mercury concentrations was between 1999-2000 and the subsequent releases. The decreasing trend in the ratio of mercury intake to fish consumed is observed after 2000, between 2001-2002 and 2009-2010, as is shown in Figure 14. Thus this finding does not explain the change in blood mercury.

43

There are limitations of the analysis that might affect the observed relationships. The laboratory method for measuring blood total mercury changed between survey releases 2001-2002 and 2003-2004 (Table 4). Thus some of the change observed in the blood mercury data between the first four years (1999-2002) and the last 8 years (2003-2010) could be attributed in part to the laboratory method. Caldwell, et al, 2009, reported a small bias due to the change in laboratory methods. They observed a THg difference between the methods (earlier method compared to the latter method) of -17 percent in the low concentration (0.24 μg/L) quality control pool and 7 percent in the high concentration (10.6 μg/L) quality control pool (Caldwell, et al. 2009). Most observed THg concentrations are between these two test concentrations. Caldwell et al. considered a correction for methodological differences but found it had little effect on the conclusions.

The data used in the analysis do not include the quantities consumed for each meal nor the mercury content of the fish item that was consumed. Instead, the analysis uses geometric mean estimates of these values. As a result, the actual variation of the estimated grams of fish consumed and the 30-day mercury intake is most likely greater than estimated. Thus, the upper percentiles presented in the tables are likely to underestimate the actual quantities.

In order to calculate mercury intake, we used fish tissue mercury concentration data from the same time-period, 1999-2010, for most species, but we did not have enough data to assign mercury concentrations to fish species by NHANES survey release. Thus, if mercury in fish tissue was changing over the study period, this would not be accounted for in the analysis. Furthermore, mercury varies in water bodies across the United States and the world, but given the data limitations we do not know the source of the fish consumed by individual participants. Another factor that hampers the calculation of mercury intake is the possible changes in commercial fishing practices that affect the amount of mercury that gets into the fish at markets and grocery stores. For example, fisheries may have reduced fishing of larger fish which are generally known to contain more mercury. One improvement that could be possible in this analysis would be to adjust the mercury concentrations in fish by the market share of fish size.

An additional limitation is the NHANES survey design. Regional differences have been reported in the consumption of fish, especially between coastal and inland regions (Mahaffey et al., 2009). NHANES does not control for these regional differences from year to year. It is possible that some of the observed findings may be related in part to changes in the regional patterns in NHANES from year to year.

Another limitation lies in the use of dietary recall data. Both the 24-hour recall data and the 30-day frequency data have measurement error associated with them. This measurement error is known to reduce the power to detect relationships (Willett, 1998). The conclusion that fish consumption has changed minimally over the course of the study period relies on dietary recall data, both 24-hour recalls and food frequency questionnaires, which have known limitations such as recall bias. However, the methodology in the data collection across years is identical, thus it would be unlikely that the recall bias would change from year to year.

Finally, the statistical model assumes a linear relationship between the fish mercury intake and the blood MeHg. A detailed analysis of the data suggests a slightly non-linear relationship such that for very frequent consumers of fish, the predicted consumption is greater than the reported value. This apparent relationship may be due to participant problems estimating the number of fish meals, a nonlinear biological response to frequent fish consumption, or other factors. Assessing the functional form of the relationship is complicated by the high percentage of imputed values. Although other relationships might be modeled, the basic conclusions should not be affected.

Oken et al., 2003, found a decline in fish consumption by pregnant women between 1999-2000 and 2001-2002 in Massachusetts: they attributed this to national fish consumption advisories. This analysis does not show the same result in women of child-bearing age. This analysis found no trend over time in amount of fish consumed or frequency of fish consumed. As fish consumption did not decrease after the issuance of either the 2001 or 2004 national fish consumption advisories, we can conclude that the issuance did not influence women on a national level to decrease their fish consumption. The decrease in the ratio of mercury intake to fish consumed occurred between 2001-2002 through 2009-2010. It is possible that fish advisories have led women to choose fish of lower mercury concentrations; however, the NHANES survey is not designed to assess the effectiveness of fish advisories, thus we cannot draw this conclusion from this analysis.

The cause of the discrepancy observed in detecting a difference in blood MeHg levels between 1999-2000 and the subsequent survey releases but no corresponding difference in the frequency and amounts of fish eaten, is not yet clear. The models predicting blood mercury from mercury intake per body weight show a strong relationship between mercury intake and blood mercury concentrations. The absence of a trend in mercury intake from fish would be consistent with no significant change in blood mercury concentrations. However, other factors that affect the relationship and the uncertainty in the blood mercury measurements (reflected in part by the presence of non-detects) complicate assessment of the relationship between mercury intake and blood mercury. Even though the mercury intake per body weight is strongly related to blood mercury concentrations, there are changes in blood mercury concentrations that are not predicted by mercury intake, particularly the drop from the 1999-2000 NHANES release to the subsequent NHANES releases. This drop may be due to changes in mercury intake not reflected in the fish consumption data, changes in other factors affecting blood mercury concentrations, changes in the procedures for measuring mercury concentrations in the blood samples, or to random factors affecting the selection of NHANES subjects. The magnitude of the drop in blood mercury from the 1999-2000 NHANES release to subsequent releases relative to the uncertainty in the estimates suggests that the drop in blood mercury concentrations is unlikely to be due to chance. At the same time, none of the available predictors explain the drop, suggesting that higher levels in 1999-2000 may be due to chance or unidentified causes.

Conclusions 5

The analyses found blood mercury concentrations in NHANES survey release 1999-2000 to be significantly higher than the mean of the subsequent releases for both blood THg and blood MeHg. The geometric mean blood THg in 1999-2000 was 1.21 times higher than the geometric mean across the subsequent 10 years (2001-2010), representing an 18 percent decrease between 1999-2000 and 2001-2010. For blood MeHg, the geometric mean in 1999-2000 was 1.51 times higher than the geometric mean across the subsequent 10 years. This represents a decrease of 34 percent between 1999-2000 and 2001-2010. Additionally, the percent with THg >5.8 μg/L and MeHg >5.8 μg/L is significantly higher in survey release 1999-2000. The percentage of women of reproductive age with blood THg over 5.8 μg/L in 1999-2000 was 2.64 times that found in 2001-2010, a decrease of 62 percent between 1999-2000 and 2001-2010. For blood MeHg, the percent of women of reproductive age over 5.8 μg/L in 1999-2000 was 2.86 times higher than the percent of women in 2001-2010, representing a 65 percent decrease between 1999-2000 and 2001-2010. The analysis also found a significant quadratic trend in blood MeHg concentration since 1999-2000. This trend indicates decreasing blood MeHg concentrations between the initial sets of NHANES survey releases, followed by relatively small changes and a slight increase in the last years.

There was a significant relationship between mercury intake from fish consumption and blood mercury, although mercury intake did not fully explain the differences observed across the survey releases. The analysis showed few changes in fish consumption and mercury intake over the study period. There was a marginally statistically significant decreasing trend across NHANES survey releases in the ratio of mercury intake to fish consumed that is consistent with women shifting their consumption to fish with lower mercury concentrations; however, other studies are needed to determine 1) if there is a link between changing consumption patterns and blood mercury and 2) if fish advisories have led to the changing consumption patterns.

Demographic characteristics were associated with blood mercury as expected: higher concentrations observed with increasing age and income and higher concentrations observed in the other race category while lower concentrations observed in Mexican Americans. Similar patterns between fish consumption and demographic characteristics were found.

Adams, D.H., McMichael Jr., R.H., and Henderson, G.E. 2003. Mercury levels in marine and estuarine fishes of Florida 1989-2001. Florida Marine Research Institute. Technical Report TR-9. 2nd ed. rev. 57 pp.

Ahuja JKA, Montville JB, Omolewa-Tomobi G, Heendeniya KY, Martin CL, Steinfeldt LC, Anand J, Adler ME, LaComb RP, and Moshfegh AJ. 2012. USDA Food and Nutrient Database for Dietary Studies, 5.0. U.S. Department of Agriculture, Agricultural Research Service, Food Surveys Research Group, Beltsville, MD.

Alaska State Department of Health and Social Services, Division of Public Health. 2007. Fish consumption advice for Alaskans: a fish management strategy to optimize the public's health. Epidemiology Bulletin. Recommendations and Reports. Oct. 11(4).

Arkansas State Department of Environmental Quality. 2010. Surface water quality and fish monitoring data. Available at: http://www.adeq.state.ar.us/techsvs/water_quality/monitors.asp.

Bahnick, D., Sauer, C., Butterworth, B., Kuehl, D. 1994. A national study of mercury contamination of fish. Chemosphere 29:537-546

Björnberg, K.A., Vahter, M., Petersson-Grawé, K., Glynn, A., Cnattingius, S., Darnerud, P.O., Atuma, S., Aune, M., Becker, W., and Berglund, M. 2003. MeHg and inorganic mercury in Swedish pregnant women and in cord blood: influence of fish consumption. Environ Health Perspect 111:637–641.

Burger, J. and Gochfeld, M. 2006. Mercury in fish available in supermarkets in Illinois: Are there regional differences? Sci Total Environ. 367:1010-1016.

Caldwell, K.L., Mortensen, M.E., Jones, R.L., Caudill, S.P., Osterloh, J.D. 2009. Total blood mercury concentrations in the U.S. population: 1999-2006. Int J Hyg Environ Health. Nov;212(6):588-98.

Centers for Disease Control and Prevention (CDC) 2010a. Data and Documentation. National Center for Health Statistics (NCHS). National Health and Nutrition Examination Survey Data. Hyattsville, MD: U.S. Department of Health and Human Services, Centers for Disease Control and Prevention. http://www.cdc.gov/nchs/nhanes/nhanes_questionnaires.htm. Accessed July 31, 2010.

Centers for Disease Control and Prevention (CDC) 2010b. National Center for Health Statistics (NCHS). National Health and Nutrition Examination Survey Analytical Guidelines. Hyattsville, MD: U.S. Department of Health and Human Services, Centers for Disease

Control and Prevention. http://www.cdc.gov/nchs/nhanes/nhanes2003-2004/analytical_guidelines.htm.

Davis, J.A., A.R. Melwani, S.N. Bezalel, J.A. Hunt, G. Ichikawa, A. Bonnema, W.A. Heim, D. Crane, S. Swenson, C. Lamerdin, and M. Stephenson. 2010. Contaminants in fish from California lakes and reservoirs: technical report on a two-year screening survey. a report of the surface water ambient monitoring program (SWAMP). California State Water Resources Control Board, Sacramento, CA.

Denton, G.M. 2007. Mercury levels in Tennessee fish. Tennessee Department of Environment and Conservation. Nashville, TN. Available at: http://www.tn.gov/environment /wpc/publications /pdf/fishmercurylevels.pdf.

Health Canada, 2008. Human Health Risk Assessment of Mercury in Fish and Health Benefits of Fish Consumption. Bureau of Chemical Safety, Food Directorate, Health Products and Food Branch, Health Canada. Available at: http://www.hc-sc.gc.ca/fn-an/pubs/mercur/merc_fish_poisson-eng.php#appa

Hyndman, Rob J. and Fan, Yanan, 1996. Sample quantiles in statistical packages. The American Statistician, 50, 361-365.

Kudo, Y., Falcigila, G.A., Couch, S.C. 2000. Evolution of meal patterns and food choices of Japanese-American females born in the United States. Eur J Clin Nutr 54:665–670.

Louisiana Department of Environmental Quality. 2012. Mercury Levels in fish. Available at: http://www.deq.louisiana.gov/portal/tabid/2733/Default.aspx

Mahaffey, K., Clickner, R., Bodurow, C. 2004. Blood organic mercury and dietary mercury intake: National Health and Nutrition Examination Survey, 1999 and 2000. Environmental Health Perspectives, 112, 562-570

Mahaffey, K.R., Clickner, R.P., and Jeffries, R.A. 2009. Adult women's blood mercury concentrations vary regionally in the United States: Association with patterns of fish consumption (NHANES 1999-2004). Environmental Health Perspectives, 117(1), 47-53.

Massachusetts Department of Environmental Protection. Fish Mercury Research Data Portal. 2008, Available at: http://public.dep.state.ma.us/fish/.

McBride, D. 2005. Analysis of chemical contaminant levels in store-bought fish from Washington State. Available at: http://epa.gov/waterscience/fish/forum/2005/.

McCarty, H.B., Miller, K., Brent, R.N., and Schofield, J. 2004. Results of the Lake Michigan mass balance study: mercury data report. Prepared for U.S. EPA Great Lakes National Program Office. Available at: http://www.epa.gov/glnpo/lmmb/results/mercury/lmmbhg.pdf.

McKelvey, W., Chang, M., Arnason, J., Jeffery, N., Kricheff, J., Kass, D. Mercury and polychlorinated biphenyls in Asian market fish: a response to results from mercury biomonitoring in New York City. Environ Res. 2010 Oct;110(7):650-7. Epub 2010 Aug 6.

Mergler, D., Anderson, H.A., Chan, L.H., Mahaffey, K.R., Murray, M., Sakamoto, M., and Stern, A.H. 2007. The Panel on Health Risks and Toxicological Effects of Methylmercury. Methylmercury exposure and health effects in humans: a worldwide concern. Ambio 36:3–11.

Micro Analytical Systems, Inc. 2008. Safe Harbor News. Winter 2008.

NRC (National Research Council). Committee on the Toxicological Effects of Methylmercury. 2000. Washington, DC: National Academies Press.

Oken, E., Kleinman, K.P., Berland, W.E., Simon, S.R., Rich-Edwards, J.W., and Giillman, M.W. 2003. Decline in fish consumption among pregnant women after a national mercury advisory. Obstet Gynecol. Aug;102(2):346-51.

Rice, G., Swartout, J., Mahaffey, K., Schoeny, R., 2000. Derivation of the U.S. EPA's oral reference dose (RfD) for methylmercury. Drug Chem Toxicol. 23(1):41-54.

Rogers, John W., 2003. Estimating the variance of percentiles using replicate weights ASA Proceedings of the Joint Statistical Meetings, 3525-3532. American Statistical Association (Alexandria, VA)

Sanzo, J.M., Dorronsoro, M., Amiano, P., Amurrio, A., Aguinagalde, F.X., and Azpiri, M.A. 2001. Estimation and validation of mercury intake associated with fish consumption in an EPIC cohort of Spain. Public Health Nutr 4:981–988.

Sarndal, C.E., Swensson, B. and Wretman, J, 1992. Model assisted survey sampling. Springer-Verlag Inc (Berlin; New York)

SAS Institute Inc. 2010. SAS/STAT® 9.22 User's Guide. Cary, NC: SAS Institute Inc

Schober, S.E., Sinks, T.H., Jones, R.L., Bolger, P.M., McDowell, M., Osterloh, J., Garrett, E.S., Canady, R.A., Dillon, C.F., Sun, Y., Joseph, C.B., and Mahaffey, K.R. 2003. Blood mercury levels in US children and women of childbearing age, 1999-2000. JAMA. Apr;289(13):1667-74.

Sechena R, Liao S, Lorenzana R, Nakano C, Polissar N, Fenske R. 2003. Asian American and Pacific Islander fish consumption—a community-based study in King County, Washington. J Expo Anal Environ Epidemiol 13:256–266.

Simonin, H., Loukmas, J., Skinner, L. and Roy, K. 2008. Strategic monitoring of mercury in New York state fish. Department of Environmental Conservation, New York State. For New York State Energy Research and Development Authority. NYSERDA Report 08-11.

Stern, A.H. and Smith, A.E. 2003. An assessment of the cord blood: maternal blood methylmercury ratio: implication for risk assessment. Environ Health Perspect 111:1465-70.

Svensson, B.G., Schutz, A., Nilsson, A., Akesson, I., Akesson, B., and Skerfving S. 1992. Fish as a source of exposure to mercury and selenium. Sci Total Environ 126:61–74.

Tsuchiya, A., Hinners, T.A., Burbacher, T.M., Faustman, E.M., Mariën, K. 2008. Mercury exposure from fish consumption within the Japanese and Korean communities. J Toxicol Environ Health. 71(15):1019-31.

USDA Food and Nutrient Database for Dietary Studies, 4.1. 2010. Beltsville, MD: Agricultural Research Service, Food Surveys Research Group.

USDA Food and Nutrient Database for Dietary Studies, 3.0. 2008. Beltsville, MD: Agricultural Research Service, Food Surveys Research Group.

USDA Food and Nutrient Database for Dietary Studies, 2.0. 2006. Beltsville, MD: Agricultural Research Service, Food Surveys Research Group.

USDA Food and Nutrient Database for Dietary Studies, 1.0. 2004. Beltsville, MD: Agricultural Research Service, Food Surveys Research Group.

U.S. Food and Drug Administration (FDA). 2010. Mercury levels in commercial fish and shellfish (1990-2010). Available http://www.fda.gov/food/foodsafety/product-specificinformation/seafood/foodbornepathogenscontaminants/methylmercury/ucm115644.htm.

U.S. Food and Drug Administration (FDA). 2010. Mercury concentrations in fish: FDA monitoring program. (1990-2010). Available: http://www.fda.gov/Food/FoodSafety/Product-SpecificInformation/Seafood/FoodbornePathogensContaminants/Methylmercury/ucm191007.htm.

U.S. Environmental Protection Agency. Office of Water. 2011. National Water Program Guidance Fiscal Year 2012. Washington, DC:U.S. Environmental Protection Agency. EPA-850-K-11-001. Available at: http://www.epa.gov/planandbudget/annualplan/FY12_OW_NPM_Gdnce.pdf.

U.S. Environmental Protection Agency. 2010. Fiscal Year 2011-2015 EPA Strategic Plan. Washington, DC:U.S. Environmental Protection Agency. Available at: http://www.epa.gov/planandbudget/strategicplan.html.

U.S. Environmental Protection Agency. Mercury study report to Congress. 1997. In: An Assessment of Exposure to Mercury in the United States, Vol 4. EPA-452/R-97-006. Washington, DC: U.S. Environmental Protection Agency, Office of Air Quality Planning and Standards and Office of Research and Development.

Virginia Department of Environmental Quality. 2009. Available at: http://www.deq.state.va.us/fishtissue/fishtissue.html.

Willet, W. 1998. Nutritional Epidemiology. Second Edition. New York, NY: Oxford University Press.

Appendix A

Extended Data Tables

Table A-1. Mercury concentrations applied to fish species (μg Hg/g fresh weight)

Species	Hg concentration (μg Hg/g wet weight)
Bass	0.263
Breaded fish products	0.013
Catfish	0.107
Cod	0.089
Flatfish	0.054
Haddock	0.069
Mackerel	0.639
Perch	0.143
Pike	0.301
Pollock	0.013
Porgy	0.315
Salmon	0.041
Sardine	0.023
Sea bass	0.188
Shark	0.628
Swordfish	1.265
Trout	0.045
Tuna	0.242
Walleye	0.265
Other finfish	0.097
Finfish, not specified	0.139
Clam	0.026
Crab	0.057
Crayfish	0.028
Lobster	0.190
Mussel	0.026
Oyster	0.027
Scallop	0.017
Shrimp	0.014
Other shellfish	0.032
Shellfish, not specified	0.026

Table A-2. Distribution of blood THg concentrations (ug/L), by NHANES survey release, age, income and race/ethnicity, women aged 16-49 years, NHANES 1999-2010

	N	Arith. Mean (95% CI)	Geometric Mean (95% CI)	Selected percentiles (95% CI)				
				25th	50th	75th	90th	95th
All Women 16-49								
1999-2000	1637	1.98 (1.51,2.45)	1.01 (0.84,1.23)	0.47 (0.39,0.58)	0.99 (0.81,1.20)	2.08 (1.56,2.77)	4.81 (3.79,6.10)	7.17 (4.93,10.44)
2001-2002	1780	1.43 (1.23,1.63)	0.83 (0.74,0.93)	0.44 (0.38,0.50)	0.85 (0.77,0.93)	1.65 (1.46,1.87)	3.05 (2.69,3.46)	4.52 (3.62,5.63)
2003-2004	1599	1.35 (1.16,1.54)	0.82 (0.72,0.93)	0.43 (0.38,0.50)	0.81 (0.70,0.94)	1.56 (1.36,1.80)	3.10 (2.57,3.73)	4.35 (3.55,5.33)
2005-2006	1792	1.44 (1.26,1.63)	0.89 (0.80,0.99)	0.47 (0.40,0.55)	0.90 (0.80,1.00)	1.66 (1.42,1.94)	3.14 (2.81,3.51)	4.38 (3.70,5.18)
2007-2008	1493	1.26 (1.07,1.44)	0.79 (0.70,0.87)	0.42 (0.38,0.47)	0.77 (0.69,0.86)	1.43 (1.25,1.65)	2.73 (2.24,3.33)	3.82 (3.06,4.77)
2009-2010	1786	1.39 (1.25,1.53)	0.86 (0.77,0.95)	0.45 (0.39,0.52)	0.84 (0.74,0.94)	1.63 (1.43,1.87)	3.11 (2.85,3.39)	4.27 (3.86,4.71)
Age								
16 to 19 years	2439	0.93 (0.85,1.01)	0.55 (0.51,0.59)	0.29 (0.26,0.32)	0.54 (0.50,0.59)	1.10 (1.00,1.21)	1.99 (1.83,2.17)	2.71 (2.43,3.03)
20 to 29 years	2739	1.26 (1.16,1.36)	0.75 (0.70,0.80)	0.40 (0.38,0.42)	0.73 (0.68,0.78)	1.46 (1.36,1.58)	2.73 (2.47,3.01)	4.05 (3.50,4.67)
30 to 39 years	2495	1.67 (1.46,1.88)	0.95 (0.87,1.03)	0.50 (0.47,0.53)	0.90 (0.83,0.98)	1.84 (1.68,2.02)	3.61 (3.16,4.12)	5.53 (4.57,6.67)
40 to 49 years	2414	1.67 (1.53,1.81)	1.05 (0.99,1.11)	0.57 (0.53,0.62)	1.01 (0.93,1.09)	1.89 (1.74,2.06)	3.73 (3.34,4.17)	5.08 (4.48,5.75)
Income								
<$20,000	2216	1.12 (0.95,1.28)	0.68 (0.63,0.74)	0.39 (0.36,0.43)	0.70 (0.63,0.78)	1.25 (1.12,1.40)	2.29 (2.00,2.63)	3.02 (2.65,3.46)
$20,000 to<$45,000	2894	1.35 (1.21,1.49)	0.78 (0.72,0.83)	0.40 (0.39,0.41)	0.78 (0.72,0.83)	1.50 (1.38,1.62)	2.70 (2.36,3.09)	3.92 (3.31,4.65)
$45,000 to <$75,000	1950	1.38 (1.25,1.51)	0.83 (0.78,0.89)	0.45 (0.41,0.50)	0.81 (0.76,0.86)	1.59 (1.46,1.74)	2.96 (2.66,3.29)	4.68 (4.00,5.48)
$75,000 and over	2148	1.81 (1.65,1.97)	1.10 (1.02,1.19)	0.58 (0.53,0.63)	1.11 (1.01,1.20)	2.20 (1.96,2.48)	4.18 (3.77,4.64)	6.00 (5.19,6.93)
$20,000 and over	225	1.44 (1.10,1.79)	0.93 (0.76,1.13)	0.51 (0.42,0.63)	0.90 (0.71,1.14)	1.88 (1.28,2.75)	2.90 (2.18,3.85)	4.25 (2.47,7.32)
Refused/Don't Know	163	1.67 (0.94,2.40)	0.91 (0.66,1.25)	0.44 (0.30,0.66)	0.86 (0.67,1.09)	1.59 (1.03,2.46)	4.20 (1.84,9.59)	7.09 (4.03,12.48)
Uncalculated*	491	1.72 (1.31,2.13)	0.86 (0.69,1.09)	0.39 (0.30,0.49)	0.90 (0.68,1.18)	2.14 (1.60,2.88)	4.18 (3.17,5.51)	5.47 (3.80,7.86)
Race								
Mexican American	2589	1.03 (0.93,1.13)	0.68 (0.64,0.73)	0.40 (0.38,0.42)	0.70 (0.66,0.75)	1.20 (1.11,1.30)	1.99 (1.81,2.20)	2.87 (2.58,3.20)
Non-Hispanic Black	2230	1.57 (1.41,1.72)	1.02 (0.94,1.10)	0.60 (0.56,0.64)	1.00 (0.91,1.10)	1.78 (1.63,1.94)	3.13 (2.76,3.57)	4.42 (3.80,5.15)
Non-Hispanic White	4043	1.39 (1.27,1.51)	0.81 (0.76,0.87)	0.40 (0.39,0.42)	0.80 (0.75,0.86)	1.60 (1.48,1.72)	3.19 (2.90,3.51)	4.63 (4.11,5.20)
Other Hispanic	751	1.64 (1.19,2.08)	0.98 (0.85,1.14)	0.51 (0.42,0.62)	1.00 (0.86,1.17)	1.91 (1.65,2.20)	3.16 (2.57,3.90)	4.32 (3.56,5.23)
Other Race	474	2.74 (2.31,3.17)	1.51 (1.30,1.74)	0.69 (0.54,0.89)	1.58 (1.26,1.98)	3.54 (2.89,4.33)	6.16 (5.31,7.14)	8.68 (6.55,11.51)

Table A-3. Distribution of blood MeHg concentrations (µg/L), by NHANES survey release, age, income and race/ethnicity, women aged 16-49 years, NHANES 1999-2010

	N	Arith. Mean (95% CI)	Geometric Mean (95% CI)	Selected percentiles (95% CI)				
				25th	50th	75th	90th	95th
All Women 16-49								
1999-2000	1,637	1.84 (1.39,2.29)	0.94 (0.74,1.19)	0.40 (0.31,0.53)	0.88 (0.71,1.08)	1.88 (1.38,2.57)	4.56 (3.48,5.97)	6.95 (4.73,10.20)
2001-2002	1,780	1.28 (1.09,1.47)	0.71 (0.57,0.90)	0.35 (0.26,0.46)	0.70 (0.60,0.81)	1.44 (1.27,1.65)	2.84 (2.48,3.25)	4.29 (3.48,5.29)
2003-2004	1,599	1.08 (0.89,1.27)	0.56 (0.40,0.78)	0.26 (0.17,0.41)	0.54 (0.43,0.68)	1.20 (1.01,1.44)	2.61 (2.08,3.26)	3.83 (3.07,4.78)
2005-2006	1,792	1.14 (0.98,1.31)	0.60 (0.44,0.82)	0.27 (0.18,0.40)	0.63 (0.53,0.75)	1.33 (1.08,1.63)	2.70 (2.31,3.16)	3.96 (3.16,4.98)
2007-2008	1,493	1.01 (0.82,1.19)	0.55 (0.40,0.75)	0.26 (0.17,0.40)	0.53 (0.44,0.64)	1.08 (0.87,1.33)	2.40 (1.88,3.07)	3.47 (2.79,4.32)
2009-2010	1,786	1.20 (1.07,1.33)	0.69 (0.56,0.86)	0.33 (0.25,0.45)	0.66 (0.57,0.77)	1.40 (1.20,1.64)	2.75 (2.49,3.04)	4.02 (3.59,4.51)
Age								
16 to 19 years	2,439	0.78 (0.68,0.88)	0.43 (0.28,0.67)	0.20 (0.08,0.50)	0.40 (0.33,0.49)	0.87 (0.76,0.99)	1.71 (1.53,1.90)	2.41 (2.08,2.80)
20 to 29 years	2,739	1.08 (0.97,1.20)	0.58 (0.43,0.80)	0.27 (0.18,0.41)	0.57 (0.50,0.65)	1.23 (1.12,1.36)	2.48 (2.22,2.77)	3.82 (3.27,4.45)
30 to 39 years	2,495	1.43 (1.23,1.62)	0.73 (0.58,0.93)	0.34 (0.26,0.45)	0.72 (0.65,0.80)	1.56 (1.39,1.75)	3.34 (2.88,3.87)	4.99 (4.06,6.14)
40 to 49 years	2,414	1.42 (1.28,1.56)	0.78 (0.64,0.97)	0.39 (0.31,0.49)	0.76 (0.69,0.83)	1.57 (1.42,1.73)	3.32 (2.92,3.78)	4.65 (4.09,5.29)
Income								
<$20,000	2,216	0.92 (0.77,1.06)	0.51 (0.37,0.71)	0.26 (0.17,0.39)	0.51 (0.43,0.59)	1.00 (0.89,1.12)	1.95 (1.66,2.28)	2.79 (2.37,3.29)
$20,000 to<$45,000	2,894	1.13 (0.99,1.28)	0.58 (0.43,0.79)	0.28 (0.18,0.41)	0.57 (0.50,0.65)	1.22 (1.09,1.35)	2.41 (2.11,2.75)	3.54 (2.97,4.20)
$45,000 to <$75,000	1,950	1.16 (1.03,1.30)	0.63 (0.48,0.83)	0.31 (0.22,0.42)	0.64 (0.55,0.73)	1.27 (1.13,1.41)	2.58 (2.21,3.01)	4.25 (3.57,5.05)
$75,000 and over	2,148	1.58 (1.43,1.74)	0.87 (0.72,1.06)	0.41 (0.33,0.50)	0.87 (0.78,0.97)	1.92 (1.69,2.18)	3.82 (3.44,4.25)	5.72 (4.81,6.80)
$20,000 and over	225	1.21 (0.89,1.54)	0.70 (0.52,0.93)	0.36 (0.25,0.50)	0.64 (0.49,0.82)	1.42 (1.00,2.02)	2.74 (1.89,3.96)	4.09 (2.17,7.71)
Refused/Don't Know	163	1.44 (0.75,2.13)	0.69 (0.47,1.02)	0.29 (0.17,0.48)	0.63 (0.44,0.90)	1.36 (0.85,2.19)	3.98 (1.63,9.72)	6.52 (3.67,11.58)
Uncalculated*	491	1.54 (1.14,1.95)	0.74 (0.54,1.03)	0.29 (0.18,0.46)	0.75 (0.55,1.02)	1.81 (1.22,2.69)	3.92 (2.93,5.24)	5.27 (3.66,7.58)
Race								
Mexican American	2,589	0.79 (0.70,0.88)	0.50 (0.36,0.70)	0.27 (0.17,0.43)	0.53 (0.46,0.61)	0.95 (0.87,1.04)	1.60 (1.45,1.76)	2.40 (2.11,2.73)
Non-Hispanic Black	2,230	1.33 (1.17,1.48)	0.78 (0.65,0.94)	0.41 (0.33,0.50)	0.79 (0.72,0.87)	1.46 (1.31,1.63)	2.77 (2.38,3.22)	4.04 (3.43,4.74)
Non-Hispanic White	4,043	1.19 (1.07,1.32)	0.62 (0.46,0.84)	0.28 (0.19,0.42)	0.60 (0.53,0.68)	1.32 (1.20,1.45)	2.85 (2.55,3.19)	4.28 (3.78,4.83)
Other Hispanic	751	1.39 (1.01,1.77)	0.78 (0.61,0.98)	0.38 (0.28,0.50)	0.80 (0.65,0.98)	1.65 (1.40,1.93)	2.76 (2.25,3.39)	4.06 (2.87,5.75)
Other Race	474	2.43 (2.05,2.82)	1.25 (1.03,1.52)	0.51 (0.39,0.67)	1.32 (1.02,1.72)	3.11 (2.52,3.84)	5.84 (4.95,6.90)	8.48 (6.42,11.21)

Table A-4. Percentages and their standard errors for categorized reports of 30-day frequency of consumption of fish, by NHANES survey release, income, race/ethnicity, and age for women aged 16-49 years, NHANES 1999-2010

Parameter	N	Percent (Standard Error)					
		0 times	1 time	2 times	3 times	4-5 times	6+ times
NHANES Survey Release							
Total Fish							
1999-2000	1,637	21.8 (2.3)	14.7 (1.1)	13.6 (1.2)	8.9 (1.6)	14.6 (1.0)	26.4 (3.0)
2001-2002	1,780	16.9 (1.1)	13.3 (1.4)	13.5 (1.6)	10.4 (1.0)	16.9 (1.2)	28.9 (1.5)
2003-2004	1,599	21.3 (1.6)	12.5 (1.7)	13.0 (1.1)	9.8 (0.9)	14.4 (1.2)	29.0 (2.0)
2005-2006	1,792	20.1 (2.2)	10.7 (1.1)	11.9 (0.8)	9.4 (0.9)	13.8 (1.1)	34.2 (3.0)
2007-2008	1,493	24.7 (1.5)	14.8 (1.0)	11.4 (0.7)	9.4 (0.9)	12.9 (1.0)	26.9 (1.5)
2009-2010	1,786	20.2 (1.9)	14.5 (0.9)	10.5 (0.6)	7.8 (0.8)	15.2 (1.1)	31.8 (1.6)
Finfish Only							
1999-2000	1,637	32.9 (1.8)	17.7 (1.1)	16.9 (0.8)	7.5 (1.9)	11.4 (1.2)	13.6 (1.9)
2001-2002	1,780	25.6 (1.5)	17.2 (1.4)	17.0 (1.5)	11.5 (0.7)	13.4 (1.4)	15.4 (1.3)
2003-2004	1,599	31.2 (2.1)	16.8 (1.3)	14.6 (0.9)	10.3 (1.0)	12.0 (1.1)	15.2 (1.4)
2005-2006	1,792	29.8 (2.6)	14.6 (1.0)	12.8 (0.7)	10.1 (0.7)	15.3 (0.9)	17.4 (2.5)
2007-2008	1,493	35.9 (1.6)	16.0 (1.2)	13.5 (0.9)	9.1 (0.7)	11.6 (1.0)	14.0 (1.3)
2009-2010	1,786	32.5 (1.9)	15.1 (1.0)	14.3 (1.2)	8.6 (1.1)	13.3 (1.3)	16.1 (1.2)
Shellfish Only							
1999-2000	1,637	48.3 (3.3)	19.4 (1.8)	9.4 (1.3)	7.0 (1.0)	9.4 (1.8)	6.5 (1.7)
2001-2002	1,780	48.3 (1.7)	17.9 (1.7)	11.8 (0.9)	7.8 (0.8)	5.6 (0.9)	8.7 (1.1)
2003-2004	1,599	48.9 (2.4)	16.5 (1.1)	11.0 (1.2)	8.6 (1.1)	7.8 (0.9)	7.2 (1.0)
2005-2006	1,792	44.4 (2.7)	17.1 (1.7)	12.9 (1.5)	6.9 (0.8)	9.3 (1.0)	9.5 (1.1)
2007-2008	1,493	49.9 (1.5)	17.0 (1.0)	11.1 (1.0)	6.9 (0.9)	7.3 (0.9)	7.8 (0.7)
2009-2010	1,786	42.2 (1.9)	17.0 (0.9)	13.7 (1.0)	9.2 (0.8)	8.2 (1.0)	9.7 (1.5)

Table A-4. Percentages and their standard errors for categorized reports of 30-day frequency of consumption of fish, by NHANES survey release, income, race/ethnicity, and age for women aged 16-49 years, NHANES 1999-2010 (continued)

Parameter	N	Percent (Standard Error)						
		0 times	1 time	2 times	3 times	4-5 times	6+ times	
Income								
Total Fish								
<$20,000	2,216	24.8 (1.5)	16.1 (0.9)	14.5 (1.1)	9.8 (1.1)	11.8 (0.8)	23.0 (1.4)	
$20,000 to<$45,000	2,894	22.9 (1.4)	14.8 (0.9)	12.4 (0.9)	9.5 (0.7)	14.4 (0.8)	26.0 (1.2)	
$45,000 to <$75,000	1,950	21.6 (1.5)	13.7 (0.9)	11.0 (0.8)	9.7 (0.8)	14.7 (1.0)	29.4 (1.6)	
$75,000 and over	2,148	16.2 (1.0)	10.3 (0.8)	12.2 (0.8)	8.5 (0.8)	16.4 (0.9)	36.3 (1.5)	
$20,000 and over	225	21.3 (3.6)	9.9 (2.5)	10.8 (3.3)	12.9 (2.6)	9.6 (2.4)	35.5 (3.8)	
Refused/Don't Know	163	20.7 (3.9)	20.9 (4.4)	13.3 (3.6)	9.0 (2.8)	9.6 (2.9)	26.4 (5.8)	
Uncalculated*	491	21.5 (2.5)	15.2 (2.2)	10.7 (2.3)	7.4 (1.7)	17.7 (2.7)	27.4 (3.8)	
Finfish Only								
<$20,000	2,216	35.7 (1.7)	19.7 (1.0)	14.9 (1.0)	7.5 (0.9)	10.7 (1.0)	11.6 (1.3)	
$20,000 to<$45,000	2,894	33.6 (1.6)	18.0 (1.0)	15.4 (1.0)	8.6 (0.6)	10.9 (0.8)	13.5 (1.1)	
$45,000 to <$75,000	1,950	31.8 (1.6)	16.2 (1.1)	15.5 (1.1)	9.2 (0.8)	11.8 (1.0)	15.5 (1.3)	
$75,000 and over	2,148	26.2 (1.2)	12.7 (0.8)	14.7 (0.9)	11.1 (0.8)	16.9 (1.1)	18.4 (1.1)	
$20,000 and over	225	31.1 (3.5)	10.6 (2.3)	11.8 (3.2)	12.9 (2.5)	10.7 (2.8)	23.0 (3.3)	
Refused/Don't Know	163	39.0 (6.8)	25.4 (4.8)	9.0 (2.2)	5.2 (2.1)	7.3 (2.4)	14.2 (5.2)	
Uncalculated*	491	32.7 (3.2)	16.6 (2.0)	12.0 (2.0)	12.6 (3.4)	12.2 (2.5)	13.9 (2.7)	
Shellfish Only								
<$20,000	2,216	55.2 (1.4)	16.2 (1.1)	9.8 (0.8)	6.0 (0.7)	5.9 (0.7)	6.9 (0.8)	
$20,000 to<$45,000	2,894	50.3 (1.6)	16.7 (0.9)	10.4 (0.8)	7.7 (0.7)	6.9 (0.8)	8.0 (0.7)	
$45,000 to <$75,000	1,950	45.8 (1.8)	17.5 (1.0)	12.8 (1.0)	8.0 (0.8)	8.8 (1.0)	7.1 (0.9)	
$75,000 and over	2,148	40.4 (1.5)	18.3 (1.2)	13.5 (0.9)	8.8 (0.7)	8.9 (1.0)	10.1 (0.9)	
$20,000 and over	225	46.6 (4.5)	16.8 (2.7)	10.4 (2.7)	7.7 (2.2)	8.9 (2.7)	9.7 (2.9)	
Refused/Don't Know	163	41.0 (4.9)	24.8 (4.4)	9.1 (2.9)	5.4 (1.8)	15.6 (4.1)	4.0 (1.6)	
Uncalculated*	491	49.2 (3.4)	19.7 (3.0)	8.9 (1.6)	6.1 (1.7)	7.4 (1.8)	8.6 (2.3)	

Table A-4. Percentages and their standard errors for categorized reports of 30-day frequency of consumption of fish, by NHANES survey release, income, race/ethnicity, and age for women aged 16-49 years, NHANES 1999-2010 (continued)

Parameter	N	Percent (Standard Error)					
		0 times	1 time	2 times	3 times	4-5 times	6+ times
Race/Ethnicity							
Total Fish							
Mexican American	2,589	22.9 (1.1)	16.9 (1.0)	15.9 (1.0)	11.8 (0.8)	14.2 (0.9)	18.3 (1.1)
Other Hispanic	751	21.1 (2.3)	20.3 (1.9)	10.2 (1.6)	9.7 (1.2)	12.3 (1.5)	26.5 (2.8)
Non-Hispanic White	4,043	21.4 (0.9)	12.9 (0.7)	12.3 (0.6)	9.2 (0.6)	14.4 (0.6)	29.8 (1.2)
Non-Hispanic Black	2,230	17.1 (1.2)	12.9 (0.8)	13.0 (0.8)	8.6 (0.7)	18.2 (1.1)	30.2 (1.2)
Other Race	474	19.5 (2.6)	7.1 (1.2)	7.2 (1.2)	7.0 (1.4)	12.6 (1.8)	46.6 (3.4)
Finfish Only							
Mexican American	2,589	38.9 (1.5)	21.4 (1.0)	15.0 (0.8)	8.7 (0.8)	8.3 (0.6)	7.8 (0.8)
Other Hispanic	751	34.7 (2.6)	20.9 (2.4)	13.9 (1.5)	7.1 (1.1)	8.4 (1.2)	15.0 (2.2)
Non-Hispanic White	4,043	31.5 (1.0)	14.9 (0.7)	15.1 (0.6)	9.6 (0.6)	13.4 (0.7)	15.5 (0.8)
Non-Hispanic Black	2,230	25.8 (1.3)	19.0 (1.1)	15.7 (0.9)	10.3 (0.8)	13.6 (0.9)	15.6 (0.9)
Other Race	474	25.7 (2.6)	11.9 (1.9)	10.7 (1.6)	10.3 (1.4)	17.2 (1.9)	24.1 (3.0)
Shellfish Only							
Mexican American	2,589	44.7 (1.6)	21.6 (1.1)	14.2 (0.9)	8.2 (0.5)	6.5 (0.7)	4.7 (0.5)
Other Hispanic	751	47.5 (3.0)	19.5 (1.7)	10.5 (1.4)	9.1 (1.2)	5.8 (1.1)	7.7 (1.2)
Non-Hispanic White	4,043	48.3 (1.2)	17.5 (0.8)	11.3 (0.6)	7.2 (0.5)	7.9 (0.6)	7.7 (0.7)
Non-Hispanic Black	2,230	45.5 (1.4)	16.3 (1.1)	12.7 (0.8)	7.4 (0.7)	8.4 (0.6)	9.6 (0.8)
Other Race	474	38.4 (3.1)	10.6 (1.7)	10.6 (1.6)	11.8 (1.8)	11.6 (1.5)	17.0 (2.2)

Table A-4. Percentages and their standard errors for categorized reports of 30-day frequency of consumption of fish, by NHANES survey release, income, race/ethnicity, and age for women aged 16-49 years, NHANES 1999-2010 (continued)

Parameter	N	Percent (Standard Error)					
		0 times	1 time	2 times	3 times	4-5 times	6+ times
Age							
Total Fish							
16 to 19 years	2,439	38.9 (1.6)	17.9 (1.2)	10.4 (0.7)	7.2 (0.7)	10.6 (0.9)	15.1 (1.1)
20 to 29 years	2,739	23.4 (1.3)	14.2 (1.0)	13.2 (0.9)	9.8 (0.9)	13.6 (1.0)	25.7 (1.4)
30 to 39 years	2,495	18.2 (1.1)	12.5 (1.0)	12.4 (0.9)	9.8 (0.7)	14.6 (0.8)	32.4 (1.4)
40 to 49 years	2,414	1.05 (1.0)	12.1 (0.8)	12.0 (0.7)	9.0 (0.7)	16.8 (0.8)	35.1 (1.3)
Finfish Only							
16 to 19 years	2,439	53.7 (1.7)	16.5 (1.1)	9.3 (0.8)	6.2 (0.7)	6.9 (0.8)	7.4 (0.8)
20 to 29 years	2,739	36.1 (1.4)	16.9 (1.0)	13.7 (0.9)	8.9 (0.7)	11.3 (0.8)	13.1 (1.1)
30 to 39 years	2,495	28.7 (1.2)	16.1 (0.9)	15.4 (0.9)	10.3 (0.7)	13.2 (0.8)	16.2 (0.9)
40 to 49 years	2,414	22.1 (1.1)	15.6 (0.9)	17.2 (1.0)	10.4 (0.8)	15.8 (0.9)	19.0 (1.2)
Shellfish Only							
16 to 19 years	2,439	58.8 (1.4)	17.9 (1.3)	9.4 (0.8)	4.7 (0.5)	4.9 (0.5)	4.3 (0.7)
20 to 29 years	2,739	47.9 (1.4)	18.2 (1.0)	11.5 (0.8)	7.6 (0.7)	7.4 (0.7)	7.4 (0.7)
30 to 39 years	2,495	43.7 (1.5)	18.1 (1.0)	11.4 (0.8)	8.2 (0.7)	8.8 (0.8)	9.7 (0.8)
40 to 49 years	2,414	45.3 (1.5)	16.0 (1.0)	12.7 (0.9)	8.4 (0.7)	8.6 (0.9)	8.9 (0.8)

Table A-5. Estimated amount of fish consumed (g) in last 30 days, by NHANES survey release, women aged 16-49 years, NHANES 1999-2010

Parameter	Years	N	Arith. Mean (95% CI)	Selected percentiles (95% CI) 25th	50th	75th	90th	95th
Amount of Fish Eaten (gm)								
Shellfish								
	1999-2000	1,637	69.3 (49.9,88.8)	0.8 (0.0,7.2)	24.1 (18.8,25.4)	88.2 (54.3,135.5)	185.8 (148.5,284.5)	284.7 (217.9,419.4)
	2001-2002	1,780	73.2 (64.0,82.4)	0.8 (0.0,4.1)	24.1 (21.8,24.8)	81.9 (68.4,92.1)	217.5 (185.3,251.1)	335.5 (285.5,419.9)
	2003-2004	1,599	66.9 (54.4,79.4)	0.5 (0.0,5.2)	24.1 (19.9,25.0)	88.5 (69.2,96.5)	191.8 (158.2,228.9)	301.8 (236.2,382.7)
	2005-2006	1,792	79.7 (70.2,89.1)	2.9 (0.0,8.6)	24.9 (23.7,30.8)	101.8 (86.8,124.8)	233.4 (199.7,255.4)	344.3 (299.3,420.2)
	2007-2008	1,493	67.2 (58.7,75.8)	0.0 (0.0,2.9)	23.4 (20.6,24.4)	78.0 (66.3,91.2)	195.9 (165.7,221.5)	312.3 (265.0,360.2)
	2009-2010	1,786	86.0 (67.3,104.7)	4.3 (0.1,8.5)	27.0 (24.7,36.5)	98.2 (85.7,126.6)	231.2 (187.3,303.0)	371.0 (287.6,530.2)
Finfish								
	1999-2000	1,637	185.2 (159.8,210.6)	21.4 (12.4,30.4)	98.9 (81.4,102.9)	238.6 (217.4,286.9)	497.5 (412.9,612.4)	684.1 (597.1,851.0)
	2001-2002	1,780	237.2 (203.7,270.8)	39.3 (30.1,43.2)	121.4 (103.0,149.4)	276.8 (255.5,317.3)	513.5 (467.7,588.5)	790.4 (722.6,924.4)
	2003-2004	1,599	203.3 (177.6,229.1)	25.2 (13.8,36.5)	101.3 (95.0,128.8)	276.6 (246.1,318.5)	524.8 (439.7,610.0)	724.2 (653.4,873.4)
	2005-2006	1,792	242.8 (204.7,280.9)	28.1 (13.5,42.0)	129.3 (100.7,159.0)	327.5 (277.3,382.3)	616.1 (526.8,744.2)	863.2 (744.2,1087.7)
	2007-2008	1,493	191.8 (167.7,215.9)	16.4 (9.2,23.5)	96.5 (70.9,104.1)	255.5 (225.5,292.5)	522.1 (466.2,572.2)	719.4 (637.9,868.8)
	2009-2010	1,786	222.5 (193.7,251.3)	22.4 (13.0,31.8)	103.0 (94.6,137.9)	315.1 (260.5,366.1)	543.0 (506.8,657.6)	829.7 (711.9,939.9)
Total Fish								
	1999-2000	1,637	254.6 (213.4,295.8)	27.2 (22.2,43.8)	136.0 (117.7,162.4)	329.7 (279.7,400.6)	663.3 (567.8,802.6)	875.9 (769.1,1073.7)
	2001-2002	1,780	310.5 (275.0,345.9)	58.7 (43.9,68.3)	169.5 (148.9,204.0)	378.9 (343.4,411.1)	717.7 (639.4,789.7)	1012.8 (874.9,1205.2)
	2003-2004	1,599	270.2 (235.3,305.2)	41.3 (22.7,58.5)	159.8 (128.2,186.7)	374.8 (321.7,414.4)	646.8 (575.6,769.7)	926.4 (836.9,1044.9)
	2005-2006	1,792	322.5 (277.1,367.8)	43.5 (23.0,69.2)	186.1 (147.7,236.9)	440.5 (377.6,524.7)	792.0 (672.9,960.9)	1085.5 (976.4,1254.7)
	2007-2008	1,493	259.0 (228.5,289.6)	24.1 (19.0,27.4)	137.5 (108.2,158.2)	357.5 (312.5,398.6)	653.7 (567.8,796.6)	940.6 (817.9,1157.5)
	2009-2010	1,786	308.5 (269.3,347.8)	38.2 (24.4,50.0)	170.1 (143.1,204.3)	424.4 (376.0,474.7)	768.0 (672.8,868.2)	1111.8 (950.5,1235.1)

Table A-6. Estimated mercury intake (µg) in last 30 days, by NHANES survey release, women aged 16-49 years, NHANES 1999-2010

Parameter	Years	N	Arith. Mean (95% CI)	25th	50th	75th	90th	95th
Intake of MeHg (µg)								
Shellfish								
	1999-2000	1,637	2.75 (1.86,3.63)	0.01 (0.00,0.10)	0.34 (0.27,0.36)	1.95 (0.88,3.47)	8.88 (4.92,13.47)	14.49 (11.50,17.61)
	2001-2002	1,780	2.71 (2.40,3.02)	0.01 (0.00,0.06)	0.34 (0.31,0.35)	1.94 (1.53,2.54)	8.76 (6.69,9.70)	13.20 (12.42,14.43)
	2003-2004	1,599	2.26 (1.73,2.80)	0.01 (0.00,0.07)	0.34 (0.28,0.35)	1.81 (1.30,2.49)	6.71 (4.48,9.58)	12.99 (9.62,16.07)
	2005-2006	1,792	2.85 (2.38,3.32)	0.04 (0.00,0.12)	0.35 (0.34,0.42)	2.57 (1.81,3.35)	9.32 (6.87,12.21)	13.60 (12.61,15.98)
	2007-2008	1,493	2.25 (1.89,2.61)	0.00 (0.00,0.04)	0.33 (0.29,0.35)	1.77 (1.31,2.44)	6.41 (4.91,9.14)	12.23 (9.87,14.23)
	2009-2010	1,786	2.77 (2.11,3.42)	0.06 (0.00,0.12)	0.38 (0.35,0.52)	2.56 (1.94,3.13)	8.48 (6.18,10.89)	13.62 (10.11,18.61)
Finfish								
	1999-2000	1,637	28.26 (23.24,33.29)	0.38 (0.22,0.53)	10.48 (8.68,11.27)	29.62 (24.77,38.29)	70.33 (57.39,96.75)	132.27 (98.82,159.01)
	2001-2002	1,780	34.68 (26.73,42.64)	0.69 (0.53,0.87)	13.81 (11.16,16.68)	38.25 (33.40,41.71)	72.02 (66.53,83.12)	125.18 (99.34,158.28)
	2003-2004	1,599	27.44 (23.68,31.20)	0.44 (0.24,0.63)	10.48 (8.85,13.32)	35.16 (30.21,39.10)	71.25 (66.23,79.73)	104.80 (87.23,122.35)
	2005-2006	1,792	29.12 (25.58,32.67)	0.49 (0.24,0.73)	13.35 (10.56,16.89)	38.57 (35.91,45.03)	71.39 (66.44,81.72)	108.62 (93.63,129.74)
	2007-2008	1,493	27.08 (22.15,32.01)	0.28 (0.16,0.41)	10.12 (8.31,10.53)	30.80 (26.46,35.89)	67.72 (58.50,86.06)	121.74 (96.42,135.42)
	2009-2010	1,786	28.65 (25.24,32.06)	0.39 (0.23,0.56)	11.91 (10.45,15.20)	36.60 (31.34,39.20)	72.39 (66.53,79.41)	109.16 (95.39,122.49)
Total Fish								
	1999-2000	1,637	31.01 (25.40,36.62)	0.39 (0.32,0.81)	11.32 (10.49,14.64)	35.94 (27.50,41.22)	79.07 (64.07,100.06)	140.17 (102.81,176.54)
	2001-2002	1,780	37.40 (29.36,45.43)	1.72 (0.78,3.18)	17.51 (13.76,20.04)	39.51 (37.86,44.32)	77.57 (70.23,91.48)	125.40 (105.30,165.19)
	2003-2004	1,599	29.70 (25.60,33.81)	0.74 (0.33,1.74)	12.20 (10.55,16.01)	37.79 (32.83,42.45)	78.40 (68.60,82.49)	105.86 (96.12,123.05)
	2005-2006	1,792	31.97 (28.14,35.81)	1.02 (0.32,3.10)	15.82 (13.69,19.13)	43.46 (38.36,49.22)	78.88 (72.25,92.35)	119.79 (102.70,132.83)
	2007-2008	1,493	29.33 (24.21,34.46)	0.34 (0.27,0.39)	10.51 (9.48,12.45)	34.38 (29.83,38.31)	73.86 (61.59,97.82)	128.48 (103.75,141.44)
	2009-2010	1,786	31.42 (27.83,35.00)	0.57 (0.35,1.42)	14.54 (11.42,17.40)	39.40 (36.14,44.76)	79.40 (72.04,85.56)	118.68 (98.00,130.99)

Table A-7. Estimated mercury intake per unit body weight (µg Hg/kg bw) in last 30 days, by NHANES survey release, women aged 16-49 years, NHANES 1999-2010

Parameter	Years	N	Arith. Mean (95% CI)	Selected percentiles (95% CI)				
				25th	50th	75th	90th	95th
Intake of MeHg per Unit Body weight (µg/kg)								
Shellfish								
	1999-2000	1,637	0.04 (0.03,0.05)	0.00 (0.00,0.00)	0.00 (0.00,0.01)	0.03 (0.01,0.05)	0.12 (0.07,0.18)	0.20 (0.17,0.28)
	2001-2002	1,780	0.04 (0.03,0.04)	0.00 (0.00,0.00)	0.00 (0.00,0.00)	0.03 (0.02,0.04)	0.11 (0.10,0.14)	0.20 (0.17,0.24)
	2003-2004	1,599	0.03 (0.02,0.04)	0.00 (0.00,0.00)	0.00 (0.00,0.01)	0.02 (0.02,0.03)	0.10 (0.07,0.14)	0.19 (0.14,0.26)
	2005-2006	1,792	0.04 (0.04,0.05)	0.00 (0.00,0.00)	0.00 (0.00,0.01)	0.04 (0.03,0.05)	0.13 (0.10,0.16)	0.22 (0.18,0.26)
	2007-2008	1,493	0.03 (0.03,0.04)	0.00 (0.00,0.00)	0.00 (0.00,0.00)	0.02 (0.02,0.03)	0.10 (0.07,0.13)	0.17 (0.14,0.23)
	2009-2010	1,786	0.04 (0.03,0.05)	0.00 (0.00,0.00)	0.01 (0.00,0.01)	0.03 (0.03,0.05)	0.11 (0.09,0.16)	0.21 (0.16,0.28)
Finfish								
	1999-2000	1,637	0.41 (0.33,0.49)	0.00 (0.00,0.00)	0.15 (0.12,0.17)	0.41 (0.37,0.48)	1.01 (0.82,1.40)	1.81 (1.39,2.59)
	2001-2002	1,780	0.50 (0.38,0.63)	0.00 (0.00,0.01)	0.20 (0.17,0.24)	0.55 (0.48,0.59)	1.07 (0.97,1.20)	1.65 (1.45,2.22)
	2003-2004	1,599	0.40 (0.34,0.47)	0.00 (0.00,0.00)	0.15 (0.13,0.18)	0.47 (0.40,0.57)	1.02 (0.87,1.20)	1.59 (1.33,1.95)
	2005-2006	1,792	0.42 (0.36,0.47)	0.00 (0.00,0.01)	0.19 (0.16,0.23)	0.56 (0.51,0.63)	1.05 (0.90,1.22)	1.60 (1.31,1.99)
	2007-2008	1,493	0.39 (0.31,0.46)	0.00 (0.00,0.00)	0.13 (0.10,0.15)	0.43 (0.38,0.47)	1.01 (0.87,1.26)	1.65 (1.34,2.14)
	2009-2010	1,786	0.41 (0.36,0.47)	0.00 (0.00,0.00)	0.17 (0.14,0.21)	0.50 (0.42,0.58)	1.06 (0.97,1.19)	1.57 (1.39,1.89)
Total Fish								
	1999-2000	1,637	0.45 (0.36,0.54)	0.01 (0.00,0.01)	0.17 (0.15,0.20)	0.46 (0.40,0.56)	1.13 (0.95,1.43)	2.02 (1.43,2.73)
	2001-2002	1,780	0.54 (0.41,0.67)	0.02 (0.01,0.05)	0.24 (0.20,0.28)	0.59 (0.54,0.64)	1.13 (1.04,1.30)	1.68 (1.52,2.27)
	2003-2004	1,599	0.44 (0.37,0.51)	0.01 (0.00,0.02)	0.17 (0.15,0.21)	0.52 (0.44,0.60)	1.10 (0.90,1.28)	1.67 (1.39,2.01)
	2005-2006	1,792	0.46 (0.39,0.52)	0.02 (0.00,0.05)	0.23 (0.19,0.28)	0.61 (0.55,0.67)	1.16 (0.99,1.30)	1.75 (1.47,2.10)
	2007-2008	1,493	0.42 (0.34,0.49)	0.00 (0.00,0.01)	0.15 (0.12,0.17)	0.47 (0.42,0.53)	1.10 (0.93,1.43)	1.71 (1.45,2.33)
	2009-2010	1,786	0.45 (0.40,0.51)	0.01 (0.00,0.02)	0.20 (0.17,0.24)	0.55 (0.47,0.64)	1.15 (1.05,1.29)	1.69 (1.47,2.00)

Table A-8. Estimated amounts consumed in last 30 days; amount of fish consumed (g), mercury intake (µg), and mercury intake per unit body weight (µg/kg), by income, race/ethnicity, and age, women aged 16-49 years, NHANES 1999-2010

Parameter	N	Arith. Mean (95% CI)	Selected percentiles (95% CI)				
			25th	50th	75th	90th	95th
Amount of Fish Eaten (gm)							
Income							
<$20,000	2,216	243.5 (216.5,270.5)	23.8 (18.1,39.8)	118.2 (100.7,134.1)	318.4 (275.0,362.8)	630.8 (546.1,688)	926.5 (780.5,1103)
$20,000 to<$45,000	2,894	266.0 (243.0,289.1)	26.8 (21.9,42.8)	139.3 (126.9,159.0)	338.5 (310.3,375.8)	653.0 (585.1,759)	1025 (884.7,1152)
$45,000 to <$75,000	1,950	288.3 (257.0,319.6)	28.3 (24.3,43.5)	157.4 (137.5,181.0)	364.7 (331.8,403.1)	701.4 (632.0,779.9)	929.1 (846.8,1075)
$75,000 and over	2,148	326.6 (305.2,347.9)	63.7 (44.7,69.2)	217.1 (194.0,229.1)	462.1 (427.1,495.4)	769.4 (710.7,837.8)	1008 (942.6,1106)
$20,000 and over	225	343.3 (276.5,410.0)	42.4 (16.2,70.4)	202.8 (125.4,274.3)	509.9 (456.2,672.5)	784.5 (697.0,1180)	1167 (853.8,1534)
Refused/Don't Know	163	283.2 (155.0,411.5)	27.5 (10.9,60.6)	115.3 (73.2,182.6)	347.9 (201.9,604.1)	805.9 (469.6,1579)	1353 (702.4,2276)
Uncalculated*	491	285.6 (228.6,342.7)	26.5 (17.9,59.6)	158.5 (122.2,195.4)	373.1 (286.1,496.8)	690.3 (603.1,981.9)	1021 (799.7,1506)
Race/Ethnicity							
Mexican American	2,589	268.6 (244.9,292.2)	34.1 (28.8,41.5)	148.2 (136.7,150.2)	343.8 (321.2,380.3)	649.9 (596.7,725.4)	982.5 (883.1,1155)
Other Hispanic	751	282.3 (235.1,329.5)	29.1 (19.4,49.1)	139.3 (106.9,175.1)	377.2 (284.5,468.4)	741.5 (622.5,876.4)	1040 (862.2,1530)
Non-Hispanic White	4,043	270.8 (252.0,289.5)	34.4 (24.5,43.4)	158.3 (138.6,162.5)	370.9 (343.8,400.3)	673.6 (628.4,731.0)	923.6 (856.8,992.0)
Non-Hispanic Black	2,230	315.0 (292.0,337.9)	59.1 (55.8,66.7)	181.7 (168.8,199.3)	396.0 (373.0,436.9)	756.7 (682.9,831.6)	1101 (989.0,1212)
Other Race	474	448.8 (348.5,549.2)	59.3 (22.9,99.7)	268.9 (209.4,339.2)	583.8 (511.3,683.4)	1065 (885.0,1285)	1412 (1177,1786)
Age							
16 to 19 years	2,439	160.3 (141.0,179.5)	6.70 (3.00,10.5)	53.6 (42.5,64.9)	197.5 (168.0,222.8)	434.6 (390.7,506.9)	687.2 (609.0,763.6)
20 to 29 years	2,739	253.3 (232.4,274.2)	24.8 (21.7,37.9)	129.4 (115.2,148.7)	340.7 (297.3,380.5)	653.5 (583.3,733.1)	941.6 (866.5,1058)
30 to 39 years	2,495	310.0 (286.7,333.3)	55.8 (42.5,60.9)	179.8 (159.7,198.8)	411.3 (377.1,445.3)	731.8 (667.2,804.3)	1031 (952.3,1112)
40 to 49 years	2,414	339.5 (311.5,367.6)	69.1 (59.1,83.9)	215.9 (194.9,229.8)	456.2 (420.2,496.1)	781.6 (720.8,856.8)	1075 (951.3,1212)
Intake of MeHg (µg)							
Income							
<$20,000	2,216	25.61 (21.95,29.28)	0.34 (0.26,0.66)	10.49 (8.95,11.39)	29.15 (25.02,34.43)	66.09 (57.05,74.27)	106.7 (87.62,133.1)
$20,000 to<$45,000	2,894	29.27 (25.90,32.64)	0.38 (0.31,0.75)	11.41 (10.50,13.76)	34.73 (30.62,37.86)	72.69 (66.39,82.84)	123.2 (104.3,151.6)
$45,000 to <$75,000	1,950	31.83 (25.50,38.15)	0.40 (0.34,0.85)	12.77 (10.83,15.18)	38.39 (34.57,41.69)	76.57 (69.68,83.72)	110.5 (96.38,134.9)
$75,000 and over	2,148	36.40 (33.60,39.20)	2.80 (1.67,3.62)	19.70 (17.10,22.33)	47.37 (43.67,51.93)	85.32 (79.45,92.51)	128.5 (116.7,139.6)
$20,000 and over	225	36.52 (30.20,42.83)	0.90 (0.23,3.88)	21.14 (10.85,29.14)	52.97 (41.46,66.04)	95.91 (81.86,124.7)	126.6 (113.6,202.3)
Refused/Don't Know	163	38.73 (16.38,61.09)	0.39 (0.15,1.58)	7.07 (1.67,13.40)	33.57 (13.92,71.35)	107.0 (56.98,372.4)	242.4 (89.55,512.8)
Uncalculated*	491	34.37 (22.25,46.49)	0.38 (0.25,1.83)	12.18 (10.35,16.09)	39.88 (30.32,45.34)	80.78 (54.44,116.4)	137.1 (92.39,405.5)
Race/Ethnicity							
Mexican American	2,589	27.68 (24.75,30.61)	0.48 (0.41,0.66)	12.82 (9.52,14.13)	35.99 (34.59,37.81)	71.95 (63.07,79.72)	109.1 (93.60,137.3)
Other Hispanic	751	31.15 (24.90,37.39)	0.42 (0.28,0.88)	11.88 (9.84,13.00)	34.08 (28.35,44.44)	87.74 (76.42,95.78)	124.2 (98.13,157.1)
Non-Hispanic White	4,043	30.98 (28.62,33.35)	0.62 (0.35,0.81)	13.34 (11.54,15.21)	38.42 (37.01,40.53)	74.64 (69.87,81.13)	118.4 (105.6,132.5)
Non-Hispanic Black	2,230	31.09 (28.44,33.74)	1.92 (0.90,2.81)	13.68 (12.34,15.82)	37.07 (32.70,41.60)	76.19 (68.49,84.95)	119.3 (107.1,134.3)
Other Race	474	49.47 (27.83,71.10)	1.94 (0.32,5.86)	21.06 (16.29,27.28)	51.31 (43.76,67.69)	105.7 (86.12,138.9)	148.3 (125.9,184.3)

Table A-8. Estimated amounts consumed in last 30 days; amount of fish consumed (g), mercury intake (µg), and mercury intake per unit body weight (µg/kg), by income, race/ethnicity, and age, women aged 16-49 years, NHANES 1999-2010 (continued)

Parameter	N	Arith. Mean (95% CI)	Selected percentiles (95% CI)				
			25th	50th	75th	90th	95th
Intake of MeHg (µg) continued							
Age							
16 to 19 years	2,439	17.70 (15.19,20.22)	0.10 (0.04,0.15)	1.49 (0.77,2.75)	19.19 (15.61,22.64)	51.94 (43.43,61.30)	80.79 (69.24,102.8)
20 to 29 years	2,739	27.90 (25.09,30.72)	0.35 (0.31,0.57)	11.24 (10.50,12.56)	35.79 (32.48,38.39)	71.95 (66.32,81.72)	106.4 (96.85,126.4)
30 to 39 years	2,495	34.69 (31.09,38.29)	1.12 (0.74,1.81)	16.02 (13.30,18.55)	40.63 (37.40,44.60)	79.98 (71.63,91.55)	131.8 (115.7,148.0)
40 to 49 years	2,414	37.26 (32.44,42.08)	3.72 (2.70,6.09)	18.89 (17.05,20.91)	44.29 (40.92,48.79)	85.79 (79.80,93.22)	131.4 (118.2,145.3)
Intake of MeHg per Unit Body weight (µg/kg)							
Income							
<$20,000	2,216	0.36 (0.30,0.41)	0.00 (0.00,0.01)	0.13 (0.11,0.15)	0.41 (0.36,0.45)	0.94 (0.84,1.12)	1.48 (1.26,2.10)
$20,000 to<$45,000	2,894	0.42 (0.37,0.47)	0.01 (0.00,0.01)	0.17 (0.15,0.19)	0.46 (0.41,0.52)	1.05 (0.90,1.21)	1.80 (1.57,2.00)
$45,000 to <$75,000	1,950	0.46 (0.36,0.55)	0.01 (0.00,0.01)	0.18 (0.15,0.21)	0.53 (0.47,0.59)	1.04 (0.96,1.20)	1.63 (1.33,1.93)
$75,000 and over	2,148	0.54 (0.49,0.58)	0.04 (0.02,0.05)	0.27 (0.25,0.31)	0.67 (0.61,0.73)	1.27 (1.14,1.42)	1.87 (1.67,2.17)
$20,000 and over	225	0.52 (0.42,0.62)	0.01 (0.00,0.05)	0.29 (0.18,0.34)	0.80 (0.55,1.20)	1.36 (1.21,1.78)	1.69 (1.39,3.73)
Refused/Don't Know	163	0.61 (0.26,0.96)	0.01 (0.00,0.02)	0.10 (0.02,0.21)	0.40 (0.21,1.18)	2.02 (0.78,5.83)	3.83 (1.52,7.79)
Uncalculated*	491	0.52 (0.31,0.73)	0.01 (0.00,0.03)	0.18 (0.15,0.23)	0.56 (0.40,0.74)	1.08 (0.81,1.61)	1.66 (1.28,6.61)
Race/Ethnicity							
Mexican American	2,589	0.40 (0.36,0.45)	0.01 (0.00,0.01)	0.17 (0.13,0.19)	0.50 (0.45,0.55)	1.00 (0.90,1.17)	1.65 (1.47,2.03)
Other Hispanic	751	0.47 (0.36,0.57)	0.01 (0.00,0.01)	0.16 (0.12,0.22)	0.53 (0.44,0.62)	1.21 (1.07,1.44)	1.85 (1.44,2.73)
Non-Hispanic White	4,043	0.45 (0.41,0.49)	0.01 (0.01,0.01)	0.19 (0.18,0.21)	0.54 (0.49,0.58)	1.10 (1.01,1.19)	1.68 (1.56,1.84)
Non-Hispanic Black	2,230	0.40 (0.36,0.43)	0.02 (0.01,0.04)	0.17 (0.15,0.20)	0.45 (0.41,0.51)	0.98 (0.87,1.09)	1.51 (1.41,1.77)
Other Race	474	0.81 (0.47,1.15)	0.03 (0.01,0.09)	0.34 (0.25,0.44)	0.86 (0.74,1.05)	1.76 (1.38,2.23)	2.52 (2.05,3.64)
Age							
16 to 19 years	2,439	0.29 (0.25,0.33)	0.00 (0.00,0.00)	0.02 (0.01,0.04)	0.29 (0.23,0.37)	0.81 (0.72,0.95)	1.38 (1.15,1.69)
20 to 29 years	2,739	0.42 (0.37,0.47)	0.00 (0.00,0.01)	0.17 (0.15,0.19)	0.50 (0.45,0.55)	1.13 (1.01,1.25)	1.63 (1.52,1.80)
30 to 39 years	2,495	0.50 (0.44,0.55)	0.01 (0.01,0.02)	0.22 (0.19,0.25)	0.58 (0.52,0.63)	1.13 (1.04,1.29)	1.86 (1.62,2.17)
40 to 49 years	2,414	0.52 (0.44,0.59)	0.05 (0.04,0.07)	0.25 (0.23,0.27)	0.59 (0.56,0.65)	1.20 (1.09,1.35)	1.86 (1.64,2.16)

Table A-9. Blood MeHg concentrations (ug/L), by frequency of consuming fish, by NHANES survey release, women aged 16-49 years, NHANES 1999-2010

Survey release	Times eaten in 30 days	N	Arith. Mean (95% CI)	Selected percentiles (95% CI)				
				25th	50th	75th	90th	95th
1999-2000								
	0	428	0.60 (0.50,0.71)	0.21 (0.12,0.39)	0.36 (0.27,0.47)	0.69 (0.56,0.85)	1.32 (1.08,1.61)	1.74 (1.31,2.31)
	1	279	1.01 (0.72,1.30)	0.37 (0.25,0.53)	0.70 (0.54,0.90)	1.18 (0.79,1.75)	2.12 (1.27,3.53)	3.11 (1.69,5.71)
	2	223	1.17 (0.93,1.40)	0.38 (0.27,0.53)	0.78 (0.58,1.04)	1.54 (1.30,1.83)	2.50 (1.75,3.57)	3.55 (2.59,4.86)
	3	154	2.06 (0.26,3.86)	0.46 (0.16,1.33)	0.90 (0.60,1.37)	1.40 (0.49,4.02)	3.77 (0.86,16.40)	10.87 (3.09,38.27)
	4-5	227	2.27 (1.74,2.80)	0.67 (0.54,0.82)	1.22 (0.89,1.67)	2.83 (1.88,4.27)	5.69 (4.43,7.29)	7.10 (5.50,9.17)
	6 and up	326	3.36 (2.75,3.97)	1.02 (0.81,1.30)	1.91 (1.52,2.41)	4.38 (3.60,5.34)	8.33 (6.28,11.07)	11.81 (10.29,13.54)
2001-2002								
	0	401	0.43 (0.33,0.54)	0.16 (0.05,0.49)	0.29 (0.21,0.41)	0.55 (0.42,0.72)	0.92 (0.77,1.09)	1.19 (0.97,1.46)
	1	248	0.71 (0.53,0.90)	0.30 (0.19,0.46)	0.48 (0.38,0.60)	0.79 (0.63,1.01)	1.52 (0.95,2.43)	2.02 (1.41,2.89)
	2	250	0.84 (0.67,1.01)	0.32 (0.22,0.46)	0.57 (0.43,0.77)	1.10 (0.85,1.42)	1.76 (1.38,2.25)	2.14 (1.21,3.76)
	3	188	1.14 (0.78,1.50)	0.37 (0.23,0.59)	0.77 (0.58,1.01)	1.31 (1.05,1.63)	2.50 (1.33,4.70)	3.22 (1.78,5.83)
	4-5	274	1.20 (0.99,1.42)	0.44 (0.34,0.58)	0.85 (0.68,1.06)	1.60 (1.24,2.06)	2.58 (1.96,3.39)	3.44 (2.73,4.35)
	6 and up	419	2.33 (1.92,2.75)	0.73 (0.62,0.86)	1.41 (1.28,1.55)	2.82 (2.53,3.14)	5.69 (4.27,7.59)	7.16 (5.04,10.18)
2003-2004								
	0	365	0.38 (0.27,0.50)	0.14 (0.03,0.57)	0.25 (0.16,0.40)	0.44 (0.34,0.57)	0.79 (0.57,1.10)	1.19 (0.76,1.85)
	1	237	0.50 (0.36,0.65)	0.15 (0.07,0.34)	0.33 (0.20,0.53)	0.57 (0.38,0.85)	1.07 (0.70,1.63)	1.40 (0.80,2.46)
	2	205	0.65 (0.52,0.78)	0.26 (0.15,0.46)	0.47 (0.36,0.61)	0.77 (0.64,0.93)	1.43 (1.03,2.00)	2.05 (1.29,3.26)
	3	162	0.89 (0.69,1.08)	0.31 (0.20,0.46)	0.54 (0.44,0.66)	1.13 (0.81,1.58)	1.92 (1.37,2.68)	3.09 (2.19,4.35)
	4-5	241	1.15 (1.00,1.29)	0.41 (0.29,0.58)	0.76 (0.63,0.92)	1.33 (1.12,1.57)	2.57 (1.81,3.65)	4.19 (2.63,6.67)
	6 and up	389	2.07 (1.68,2.46)	0.64 (0.51,0.81)	1.21 (0.99,1.48)	2.61 (1.92,3.54)	4.36 (3.20,5.92)	6.24 (3.62,10.77)

A-14

Table A-9. Blood MeHg concentrations (ug/L), by frequency of consuming fish, by NHANES survey release, women aged 16-49 years, NHANES 1999-2010 (continued)

Survey release	Times eaten in 30 days	N	Arith. Mean (95% CI)	Selected percentiles (95% CI)					
				25th	50th	75th	90th	95th	
2005-2006									
	0	433	0.37 (0.25,0.48)	0.11 (0.03,0.39)	0.22 (0.12,0.38)	0.45 (0.33,0.61)	0.77 (0.60,0.98)	1.10 (0.83,1.46)	
	1	248	0.64 (0.50,0.78)	0.20 (0.10,0.38)	0.42 (0.32,0.57)	0.80 (0.63,1.01)	1.33 (1.00,1.77)	1.77 (1.14,2.76)	
	2	224	0.82 (0.63,1.01)	0.26 (0.16,0.41)	0.50 (0.39,0.64)	0.97 (0.80,1.17)	1.61 (1.12,2.31)	2.65 (1.25,5.60)	
	3	173	1.06 (0.68,1.45)	0.32 (0.20,0.49)	0.62 (0.47,0.81)	1.11 (0.64,1.91)	2.72 (1.28,5.79)	3.22 (1.85,5.60)	
	4-5	235	1.28 (0.82,1.73)	0.40 (0.26,0.61)	0.76 (0.62,0.93)	1.45 (1.14,1.84)	2.45 (1.16,5.16)	3.86 (1.38,10.76)	
	6 and up	479	1.84 (1.61,2.08)	0.64 (0.56,0.75)	1.20 (1.01,1.44)	2.38 (2.00,2.83)	4.07 (3.34,4.95)	5.77 (4.31,7.73)	
2007-2008									
	0	374	0.36 (0.25,0.47)	0.15 (0.05,0.41)	0.25 (0.16,0.39)	0.43 (0.34,0.53)	0.67 (0.54,0.83)	0.96 (0.72,1.29)	
	1	251	0.69 (0.45,0.92)	0.23 (0.13,0.40)	0.43 (0.31,0.60)	0.72 (0.49,1.06)	1.43 (0.99,2.08)	1.92 (1.05,3.50)	
	2	190	0.69 (0.52,0.86)	0.27 (0.17,0.43)	0.46 (0.35,0.60)	0.72 (0.60,0.88)	1.14 (0.72,1.82)	1.89 (1.21,2.96)	
	3	136	0.82 (0.57,1.07)	0.31 (0.19,0.49)	0.54 (0.42,0.69)	0.84 (0.66,1.05)	1.68 (0.93,3.02)	2.51 (1.18,5.34)	
	4-5	197	1.05 (0.87,1.23)	0.45 (0.34,0.60)	0.79 (0.62,1.01)	1.32 (1.16,1.49)	1.83 (1.51,2.21)	2.34 (1.22,4.49)	
	6 and up	345	1.95 (1.54,2.37)	0.64 (0.50,0.82)	1.24 (0.94,1.62)	2.61 (2.10,3.24)	4.21 (2.96,5.99)	6.72 (4.49,10.06)	
2009-2010									
	0	413	0.50 (0.40,0.60)	0.19 (0.08,0.45)	0.31 (0.22,0.42)	0.56 (0.48,0.66)	1.01 (0.73,1.39)	1.41 (1.13,1.75)	
	1	250	0.58 (0.50,0.67)	0.25 (0.16,0.40)	0.43 (0.34,0.54)	0.76 (0.63,0.93)	1.19 (1.02,1.38)	1.51 (1.20,1.91)	
	2	213	0.81 (0.67,0.94)	0.33 (0.23,0.46)	0.55 (0.46,0.67)	1.05 (0.76,1.46)	1.68 (1.45,1.93)	2.06 (1.50,2.82)	
	3	132	0.87 (0.70,1.04)	0.34 (0.24,0.48)	0.56 (0.43,0.73)	1.00 (0.74,1.33)	2.01 (1.36,2.97)	2.53 (1.96,3.26)	
	4-5	258	1.27 (1.05,1.50)	0.47 (0.37,0.60)	0.80 (0.61,1.06)	1.55 (1.20,2.00)	2.60 (2.23,3.03)	3.15 (2.29,4.35)	
	6 and up	520	2.11 (1.87,2.35)	0.77 (0.66,0.91)	1.36 (1.15,1.61)	2.72 (2.49,2.98)	4.24 (3.54,5.08)	6.47 (5.61,7.47)	

Table A-10. Parameter estimates and odds ratios from the logistic model predicting the probability of reporting any fish consumption in the previous 30 days

	Parameter	Std. Error	p-Value	Odds Ratio
Intercept	1.3809	0.08	<0.0001	
Age, Overall			<0.0001	
Age	1.1679	0.09	<0.0001	
Age^2	-0.9182	0.36	0.0110	
Income, Overall			<0.0001	
0 to 20K	-0.1915	0.10	0.05	0.83
20 to 45K	-0.1201	0.08	0.15	0.89
45 to 75K	-0.0676	0.09	0.45	0.93
>75K	0.3070	0.08	0.0001	1.36
MultiHH	-0.0142	0.14	0.92	0.99
Refuse/DK	0.0683	0.23	0.77	1.07
Over 20K	0.0181	0.19	0.92	1.02
Race, Overall			0.0001	
Non-Hispanic Black	0.2510	0.09	0.0060	1.29
Mexican Amer.	-0.0926	0.07	0.20	0.91
Other Hispanic	-0.0261	0.11	0.82	0.97
Other Race	0.0533	0.14	0.70	1.05
Non-Hispanic White	-0.1856	0.06	0.0022	0.83
NHANES Survey Release, linear trend	-0.0184	0.01	0.21	

Table A-11. Parameter estimates and relative ratios from the model predicting the frequency of fish consumption in the previous 30 days (times)

	Parameter	Std. Error	p-Value	Odds Ratio
Intercept	1.3581	0.03	<0.0001	
Age, Overall			<0.0001	
Age	0.3129	0.04	<0.0001	
Age^2	-0.4643	0.13	0.0004	
Income, Overall			<0.0001	
0 to 20K	-0.1101	0.04	0.0026	0.90
20 to 45K	-0.0388	0.04	0.28	0.96
45 to 75K	-0.0062	0.03	0.85	0.99
>75K	0.1220	0.04	0.0011	1.13
MultiHH	0.0169	0.07	0.81	1.02
Refuse/DK	-0.1535	0.12	0.19	0.86
Over 20K	0.1698	0.07	0.0136	1.19
Race, Overall			<0.0001	
Non-Hispanic Black	0.0371	0.03	0.22	1.04
Mexican Amer.	-0.2516	0.03	<0.0001	0.78
Other Hispanic	-0.1389	0.05	0.0066	0.87
Other Race	0.4057	0.06	<0.0001	1.50
Non-Hispanic White	-0.0524	0.03	0.07	0.95
NHANES Survey Release, linear trend	0.0052	0.01	0.37	

Table A-12. Parameter estimates and relative ratios from the model predicting the amount of fish consumed in a meal (meal size) (g)

	Parameter	Std. Error	p-Value	Odds Ratio
Intercept	4.0657	0.01	<0.0001	
Age, Overall			<0.0001	
Age	0.1365	0.01	<0.0001	
Age^2	-0.0338	0.05	0.48	
Income, Overall			0.39	
0 to 20K	0.0165	0.01	0.23	1.02
20 to 45K	-0.0074	0.01	0.49	0.99
45 to 75K	-0.0124	0.01	0.31	0.99
>75K	0.0088	0.01	0.52	1.01
MultiHH	0.0085	0.03	0.74	1.01
Refuse/DK	-0.0381	0.04	0.36	0.96
Over 20K	0.0241	0.03	0.35	1.02
Race, Overall			<0.0001	
Non-Hispanic Black	-0.0407	0.01	0.0003	0.96
Mexican Amer.	0.1964	0.01	<0.0001	1.22
Other Hispanic	-0.0129	0.02	0.51	0.99
Other Race	-0.0477	0.02	0.0022	0.95
Non-Hispanic White	-0.0952	0.01	<0.0001	0.91
NHANES Survey Release, linear trend	-0.0013	0.002	0.46	

Table A-13. Parameter estimates and relative ratios from the model predicting the mercury concentration of the fish consumed (µg)

	Parameter	Std. Error	p-Value	Odds Ratio
Intercept	-2.6518	0.03	<0.0001	
Age, Overall			0.0006	
Age	0.1574	0.04	0.0003	
Age^2	-0.2172	0.13	0.09	
Income, Overall			0.21	
0 to 20K	-0.0047	0.04	0.90	1.00
20 to 45K	-0.0183	0.03	0.58	0.98
45 to 75K	-0.0002	0.04	1.00	1.00
>75K	0.0409	0.04	0.28	1.04
MultiHH	-0.0259	0.07	0.71	0.97
Refuse/DK	-0.1409	0.12	0.25	0.87
Over 20K	0.1491	0.07	0.03	1.16
Race, Overall			<0.0001	
Non-Hispanic Black	-0.0015	0.03	0.95	1.00
Mexican Amer.	-0.1032	0.03	0.0002	0.90
Other Hispanic	-0.0441	0.04	0.31	0.96
Other Race	0.0560	0.04	0.17	1.06
Non-Hispanic White	0.0928	0.02	<0.0001	1.10
NHANES Survey Release, linear trend	-0.0110	0.01	0.0352	

Table A-14. Parameter estimates and relative ratios from the model predicting the inverse of body weight (1/kg)

	Parameter	Std. Error	p-Value	Odds Ratio
Intercept	0.0950	0.01	<0.0001	
Age, Overall			<0.0001	
Age	-0.1655	0.01	<0.0001	
Age^2	0.1410	0.04	0.0004	
Income, Overall			<0.0001	
0 to 20K	-0.0437	0.01	<0.0001	0.96
20 to 45K	-0.0177	0.01	0.03	0.98
45 to 75K	-0.0084	0.01	0.42	0.99
>75K	0.0378	0.01	0.0002	1.04
MultiHH	0.0142	0.02	0.41	1.01
Refuse/DK	0.0271	0.03	0.29	1.03
Over 20K	-0.0093	0.02	0.64	0.99
Race, Overall			<0.0001	
Non-Hispanic Black	-0.1309	0.01	<0.0001	0.88
Mexican Amer.	0.0081	0.01	0.21	1.01
Other Hispanic	0.0232	0.01	0.03	1.02
Other Race	0.1148	0.01	<0.0001	1.12
Non-Hispanic White	-0.0152	0.01	0.02	0.98
NHANES Survey Release, linear trend	-0.0015	0.001	0.20	

Table A-15. Parameter estimates and relative ratios from the model predicting mercury intake per unit body weight (µg/kg)

	Parameter	Std. Error	p-Value	Odds Ratio
Intercept	-1.4637	0.06	<0.0001	
Age, Overall			<0.0001	
Age	0.4413	0.07	<0.0001	
Age^2	-0.5742	0.23	0.0141	
Income, Overall			<0.0001	
0 to 20K	-0.1420	0.07	0.04	0.87
20 to 45K	-0.0821	0.06	0.18	0.92
45 to 75K	-0.0273	0.06	0.67	0.97
>75K	0.2095	0.07	0.0032	1.23
MultiHH	0.0137	0.13	0.92	1.01
Refuse/DK	-0.3055	0.24	0.21	0.74
Over 20K	0.3337	0.10	0.0016	1.40
Race, Overall			<0.0001	
Non-Hispanic Black	-0.1361	0.05	0.0069	0.87
Mexican Amer.	-0.1502	0.05	0.0065	0.86
Other Hispanic	-0.1726	0.09	0.06	0.84
Other Race	0.5289	0.09	<0.0001	1.70
Non-Hispanic White	-0.0699	0.04	0.09	0.93
NHANES Survey Release, linear trend	-0.0086	0.01	0.35